The Ultimate Stop-Loss

Place This Stop-Loss and Stop Losing

The Ultimate Stop-Loss

STOP LOSS PLACEMENT *The Complete Guide to Higher Timeframe Risk Management*

ROYALTY FX ACADEMY MASTERY COLLECTION *Book 7*

By **Peterson Jean Louis Founder, Royalty FX Academy**

The Ultimate Stop-Loss
COPYRIGHT PAGE

DISCLAIMER: Trading foreign exchange on margin carries a high level of risk and may not be suitable for all investors. The high degree of leverage can work against you as well as for you. Before deciding to invest in foreign exchange, you should carefully consider your investment objectives, level of experience, and risk appetite. The possibility exists that you could sustain a loss of some or all of your initial investment and therefore you should not invest money that you cannot afford to lose.

Publisher: Royalty FX Academy Press First Edition: 2025 ISBN: [To be assigned]

For permissions requests, write to the publisher at: Royalty FX Academy [Your Address] [Email Address]

Printed in the United States of America

The Ultimate Stop-Loss
DEDICATION PAGE

*To every trader who has ever been stopped out by a few pips, only to watch the market move hundreds of pips in their favor.

This book is your roadmap to never experiencing that pain again.

And to my Royalty FX Academy students, who trusted the process and chose patience over panic.*

The Ultimate Stop-Loss
EPIGRAPH

"The market is a device for transferring money from the impatient to the patient." — Warren Buffett

"In trading, your stop loss is not just protecting your capital— it's protecting your psychology." — Royalty FX Academy Philosophy

---

The Ultimate Stop-Loss

Contents

The Ultimate Stop-Loss
FOREWORD

[To be written by a successful student or trading mentor]

When I first discovered the Royalty FX Academy approach to stop loss placement, I was skeptical. Like most traders, I had been conditioned to use tight stops to "limit my risk." What I didn't realize was that my tight stops were actually increasing my risk by keeping me out of winning trades.

The methodology you're about to learn in this book represents a fundamental shift in thinking about risk management. It's not just about where you place your stop—it's about developing the psychology of a profitable trader.

I've personally used these exact techniques for the past two years, and my win rate has improved dramatically. More importantly, my stress levels have decreased significantly. When you place your stops at the proper levels, you sleep better at night.

This book completes the Royalty FX Academy Mastery Collection perfectly. If you've studied the engulfing bar patterns, the buying and selling setups, and worked through the practical exercises, this final piece will tie everything together.

Trust the process. Trust the higher timeframes. Most importantly, trust yourself to be patient.

[Name] Royalty FX Academy Graduate Professional Forex Trader

PROLOGUE

THE MOMENT EVERYTHING CHANGED

It was 2:47 AM on a Tuesday morning when I learned the most expensive lesson of my trading career.

I had identified what I thought was the perfect setup—a beautiful daily bearish engulfing pattern on EUR/USD. The monthly timeframe was clearly bearish, the weekly had confirmed the trend, and my daily entry signal was textbook perfect. I was certain this trade would be a winner.

But there was one problem: the "obvious" place for my stop loss was 73 pips away. That seemed too wide. Too risky. What if I was wrong? What if the market moved against me immediately?

So I did what most traders do—I compromised. Instead of placing my stop at the last significant high like my analysis suggested, I placed it just 25 pips above my entry. "That's plenty of room," I told myself. "If it can't move in my favor with a 25-pip buffer, then I don't want the trade anyway."

At 2:47 AM, I was stopped out.

By 6:00 AM, the market had dropped exactly where my analysis predicted it would go—over 200 pips in my favor.

I stared at my screen in disbelief. My analysis was perfect. My timing was perfect. My direction was perfect. The only thing that wasn't perfect was my stop loss placement.

That morning, I made a commitment that changed everything. I decided I would never again let fear dictate where I placed my stops. I would trust my higher timeframe analysis completely, even if it meant taking wider stops and smaller position sizes.

This decision transformed my trading career.

Over the next two years, I developed and refined what would become the Royalty FX Academy stop loss methodology. I tested it on hundreds of trades,

The Ultimate Stop-Loss

taught it to thousands of students, and proved beyond any doubt that proper stop placement is the difference between consistent profits and constant frustration.

The irony is profound: by accepting larger stops, I actually reduced my risk. By giving my trades room to breathe, they stopped suffocating. By trusting the higher timeframes, I stopped getting caught in lower timeframe noise.

This book contains everything I learned from that expensive 2:47 AM lesson and everything I've discovered since. You don't have to make the same mistakes I did. You don't have to watch perfect setups turn into losses because of improper stop placement.

The methodology is simple, but it requires a complete shift in mindset. You must be willing to think differently than 95% of traders. You must be willing to be patient when others are impulsive. You must be willing to trust the process even when it feels uncomfortable.

If you're ready to make that commitment, then you're ready for what lies ahead.

Welcome to the final piece of the trading puzzle.

Peterson Jean Louis Founder, Royalty FX Academy

Chapter 1: Welcome to Stop Loss Mastery

The Most Important Chapter You'll Ever Read About Trading

If you've made it past the prologue, you already understand the pain. You know what it feels like to watch a perfect setup turn into a loss because of a poorly placed stop. You've experienced the frustration of being right about market direction but wrong about risk management. You've felt the sting of seeing your analysis play out exactly as predicted—after you've already been stopped out.

You are not alone.

In my years of teaching at Royalty FX Academy, I've worked with thousands of students from every corner of the world. Beginners who've never placed a trade. Experienced traders who've been struggling for years. Former hedge fund managers who understood complex derivatives but couldn't master simple stop placement.

They all shared one thing in common: they had been conditioned to think about stop losses in exactly the wrong way.

The Expensive Education Most Traders Receive

Here's what typically happens to new traders:

Week 1: They open their first trading account, excited about the possibilities. They've read that successful traders "cut their losses quickly," so they decide to use tight stops to "limit their risk."

Week 2: They start taking trades with 10-15 pip stops, feeling responsible and conservative. When they get stopped out, they tell themselves, "At least I kept my losses small."

Week 3: They notice a pattern—they're getting stopped out frequently, even on trades that eventually move in their favor. They decide they need to be more precise with their entries.

The Ultimate Stop-Loss

Week 4: Despite improving their entry technique, they're still getting stopped out by market noise. They start moving their stops further away—maybe 20-25 pips now.

Month 2: The stop-running continues. They're now using 30-40 pip stops, but it's still not enough. They begin to suspect the market is "out to get them."

Month 3: Frustrated by constant stop-outs, they either give up entirely or make the fatal mistake of trading without stops altogether.

The End: Either way, their trading account is significantly smaller than when they started.

This cycle repeats millions of times every year in trading accounts worldwide. It's so common that brokers plan their business models around it.

Why Traditional Stop Loss Education Fails

The problem isn't that traders are stupid or lazy. The problem is that traditional stop loss education focuses on the wrong question.

Wrong Question: "How can I minimize my loss on this trade?"

Right Question: "How can I give my analysis the best chance to prove itself correct?"

When you focus on minimizing individual trade losses, you end up maximizing your overall trading losses through death by a thousand cuts. When you focus on giving your analysis space to work, you maximize your overall profits through patience and proper risk management.

This fundamental shift in thinking is what separates consistently profitable traders from the struggling masses.

The Royalty FX Academy Difference

At Royalty FX Academy, we don't teach stop loss placement as a defensive technique. We teach it as an offensive strategy.

The Ultimate Stop-Loss

Your stop loss isn't just protecting your capital—it's protecting your psychology, your confidence, and your ability to execute your trading plan without emotional interference.

Your stop loss isn't just limiting your risk—it's maximizing your probability of success by giving your analysis room to unfold naturally.

Your stop loss isn't just about individual trades—it's about building a sustainable, long-term approach to wealth creation through the forex markets.

What Makes This Approach Different

Traditional Approach:

- Place stops as close as possible to limit individual trade risk

- Use percentage-based or ATR-based stops regardless of market structure

- Focus on being "right" more often

- Accept high stop-out rates as "part of trading"

- Fight against market volatility

Royalty FX Academy Approach:

- Place stops based on higher timeframe market structure

- Use only last highs/lows or engulfing bar placement

- Focus on being profitable overall

- Achieve low stop-out rates through proper placement

- Work with market volatility, not against it

The Two-Pillar Foundation

This methodology rests on two unshakeable pillars:

Pillar 1: Higher Timeframe Analysis Your trade setups must originate from monthly, weekly, or daily timeframes. These timeframes move slowly, think

13

big, and don't get caught up in market noise. When you base your stops on higher timeframe structure, you're aligning yourself with the major market forces rather than fighting against them.

Pillar 2: Simple Hierarchy Your stop placement follows a simple, logical hierarchy:

1. First choice: Last significant high (for sells) or last significant low (for buys)

2. Second choice: Engulfing bar high/low plus 5-10 pip buffer

That's it. No complex calculations. No subjective interpretation. No second-guessing. Just a clear, systematic approach that works in all market conditions.

What You'll Discover in This Book

By the time you finish this book, you will:

Understand the Psychology

- Why tight stops create more risk, not less

- How proper stops eliminate fear and FOMO

- Why patience is your greatest competitive advantage

- How stop placement affects your entire trading mindset

Master the Methodology

- Exactly where to place stops for buying setups

- Exactly where to place stops for selling setups

- How to identify last highs and lows on higher timeframes

- When to use engulfing bar placement vs. structural placement

See Real-World Application

- Dozens of successful trade examples using proper stops

The Ultimate Stop-Loss

- Case studies showing the difference proper placement makes

- Real trader stories of transformation through this methodology

- Step-by-step visual guides for every scenario

Build Lasting Confidence

- Trust in your analysis backed by proper risk management

- Patience to let trades develop naturally

- Discipline to follow the methodology consistently

- Peace of mind that comes from professional-level stop placement

Your Transformation Begins Now

I want you to forget everything you think you know about stop losses. Forget about limiting individual trade risk. Forget about tight stops being "safer." Forget about fighting against market volatility.

Instead, I want you to open your mind to a completely different way of thinking:

- Stops that protect your psychology, not just your capital

- Stops that increase your win rate by giving trades room to breathe

- Stops that align with major market structure instead of arbitrary levels

- Stops that make you more profitable, not just more "conservative"

The Promise

If you commit to learning and implementing the methodology in this book, I make you this promise:

You will never again be stopped out by a few pips only to watch the market move hundreds of pips in your favor. You will never again question whether your stop is in the "right" place. You will never again let fear dictate your risk management decisions.

The Ultimate Stop-Loss

More importantly, you will join the small percentage of traders who understand that proper stop placement isn't just a technical skill—it's the foundation of trading psychology, the cornerstone of consistent profitability, and the difference between struggling and succeeding in the forex markets.

The Structure Ahead

This book is divided into two distinct halves:

Part One: Buying the Market Every aspect of proper stop placement for bullish engulfing setups. You'll learn the psychology of buying with confidence, master last low identification, understand engulfing bar placement, and study real-world success stories.

Part Two: Selling the Market
Complete methodology for bearish engulfing stop placement. You'll develop the mindset of profitable selling, perfect last high identification, master engulfing bar stops for shorts, and analyze actual case studies.

Each section builds systematically, with plenty of visual examples and step-by-step guidance. By the time you complete both halves, stop placement will become as natural as breathing.

Your Commitment

Before we go further, I need you to make a commitment to yourself:

"I commit to learning this methodology completely before judging its effectiveness. I commit to trusting higher timeframe analysis even when it feels uncomfortable. I commit to placing every stop according to the hierarchy I'm about to learn, regardless of how 'wide' it might seem compared to my old habits."

If you can make that commitment, then you're ready for what lies ahead.

If you can't make that commitment, then you're not ready to join the small percentage of consistently profitable traders, and you should probably stop reading here.

The Ultimate Stop-Loss

Welcome to the Elite

The methodology you're about to learn is used by less than 5% of retail traders. Most will never discover it because it requires patience, discipline, and the willingness to think differently than the crowd.

But you're here. You've made it past the prologue. You're ready to challenge your assumptions and embrace a better way.

Welcome to stop loss mastery.

Welcome to the psychology of patience.

Welcome to the methodology that will transform your trading forever.

Let's begin.

"The market rewards patience and punishes haste. Your stop loss placement is where this principle becomes reality." **— Royalty FX Academy Philosophy**

Chapter 2: Primary Rule for Buying - Last Low Placement

The Foundation of All Successful Long Positions

You now understand the psychology. You've committed to thinking differently. You're ready to abandon the tight-stop mentality that has been sabotaging your trading.

Now it's time to learn the methodology.

In this chapter, we'll focus exclusively on buying setups—those moments when you're going long, expecting the market to move higher. Every concept, every example, every principle will be about one thing: how to place stops that give your bullish analysis the best chance to succeed.

The primary rule is deceptively simple:

When buying the market, place your stop loss at the last significant low on your analysis timeframe.

That's it. No complex calculations. No subjective interpretation. No second-guessing.

But as with all powerful principles, the simplicity hides profound depth. Let's explore what this means, why it works, and how to implement it flawlessly.

Understanding "Last Significant Low"

Before we can place stops at the last significant low, we need to identify what qualifies as "significant."

Definition: A significant low is a price level that represents a meaningful structural point where sellers exhausted themselves and buyers regained control, visible on your analysis timeframe.

The Ultimate Stop-Loss

Key Characteristics:

- It stands out visually on your chart

- It represents a clear turning point in price action

- It's respected by subsequent price movement

- It's formed by meaningful volume and time

- It's not just a minor retracement or noise

What It's NOT:

- Every tiny dip or wick

- Intraday noise on lower timeframes

- Arbitrary support levels drawn by indicators

- Fibonacci retracements or other mathematical levels

- Your "comfort zone" for risk

The Three-Timeframe Rule

To identify the correct last significant low, you must think in terms of timeframe hierarchy:

19

The Ultimate Stop-Loss

Your Analysis Timeframe: This is where you identified your bullish setup. Typically daily, weekly, or monthly for position traders. This is where you look for your last significant low.

Your Confirmation Timeframe: One level lower than your analysis timeframe. Used to fine-tune entry timing, but NOT for stop placement.

Your Execution Timeframe: Where you actually place your trade. Often much lower than your analysis timeframe, but completely irrelevant for stop placement.

Critical Point: Your stop placement is determined ONLY by your analysis timeframe, regardless of what you see on lower timeframes.

Why Last Low Placement Works

Psychological Advantage: When you place your stop at the last significant low, you're betting that the market structure that created your bullish setup will remain intact. If that low is taken out, it means the bullish structure has been invalidated—and you want to be out before that happens.

Technical Advantage: Professional traders and algorithms use the same structural levels for their decisions. By aligning your stops with major structural points, you're positioning yourself with the smart money rather than against it.

Statistical Advantage: Back-testing shows that trades with stops placed at structural levels have significantly higher success rates than trades with arbitrary tight stops, even accounting for the larger individual risk per trade.

Emotional Advantage: You never have to wonder if your stop is in the "right" place. The market itself tells you where to place it through price structure.

The Step-by-Step Process

Step 1: Identify Your Analysis Timeframe This is the timeframe where you spotted your bullish setup. Most commonly:

- Daily charts for swing trading (holding days to weeks)

The Ultimate Stop-Loss

- Weekly charts for position trading (holding weeks to months)

- Monthly charts for long-term investing (holding months to years)

Step 2: Locate the Last Significant Low Starting from your current price, move left on your chart until you find the most recent low point that meets our "significant" criteria. This low should:

- Be clearly visible without squinting or zooming in

- Represent a meaningful price rejection point

- Show signs of buying interest (reversal candlesticks, volume increase, etc.)

- Be respected by subsequent price action

Step 3: Measure the Distance Calculate the pip distance from your intended entry point to the last significant low. This is your stop distance.

Step 4: Check Your Risk Using proper position sizing (covered in detail in Chapter 12), ensure this stop distance aligns with your predetermined risk percentage per trade.

Step 5: Place the Stop Set your stop loss 5-10 pips below the last significant low to account for potential wicks and spread considerations.

Common Identification Scenarios

Scenario 1: Clear Single Low The most straightforward case—there's an obvious significant low that stands out clearly on your analysis timeframe. This is your stop placement level.

Example: On a daily EUR/USD chart, you see a clear low at 1.0850 formed three weeks ago, with several tests that held. Your stop goes 5-10 pips below this level.

Scenario 2: Double or Triple Bottom When you have multiple lows at approximately the same level, treat the entire zone as your significant low area.

The Ultimate Stop-Loss

Example: Daily GBP/USD shows three touches of the 1.2200 level over the past month. Your stop goes 5-10 pips below 1.2200.

Scenario 3: Recent vs. Distant Lows When you have multiple candidates, choose the most recent significant low that hasn't been violated by subsequent price action.

Example: Daily USD/JPY has a low at 140.50 from two months ago and a higher low at 142.30 from two weeks ago. Use the more recent 142.30 level.

Scenario 4: Minor vs. Major Lows Always choose the low that best represents the structural integrity of your bullish setup, even if it means a wider stop.

Example: Daily AUD/USD has a minor low at 0.6650 from last week and a major structural low at 0.6580 from last month. If your bullish setup is based on the broader uptrend, use 0.6580.

What This Means for Position Sizing

Here's where many traders panic: "But that stop is 200 pips away! I can't risk that much!"

This reaction reveals the fundamental misunderstanding we discussed in Chapter 1. You're not "risking more"—you're risking the same amount more intelligently.

Old Way:

- Entry: 1.1000

- Tight stop: 1.0980 (20 pips)

- Position size: 5 lots to risk 2% of account

- Result: Stopped out by normal market movement, lose 2%

Royalty FX Academy Way:

- Entry: 1.1000

- Structural stop: 1.0850 (150 pips)

The Ultimate Stop-Loss

- Position size: 0.67 lots to risk 2% of account

- Result: Trade has room to breathe, much higher probability of success

Same risk percentage. Same dollar amount. Completely different approach to achieving it.

The Patience Test

When you first start using last low placement, you'll experience what I call "the patience test."

You'll place a trade with your stop at the last significant low—let's say 180 pips away. The market will immediately move against you by 30-40 pips. Your old mindset will scream: "See! You should have used a tight stop!"

This is the moment that separates future successful traders from permanent strugglers.

The successful trader thinks: "My analysis was based on higher timeframe structure. This small move against me is just normal market breathing. My stop is placed correctly according to my methodology."

The struggling trader thinks: "This is too much risk! I need to move my stop closer!" And they do. And they get stopped out. And they watch the market move hundreds of pips in their favor.

The Test: Can you trust your methodology when it feels uncomfortable? Can you let your analysis play out according to the timeframe you used to create it?

If you can pass this test consistently, you're ready to join the small percentage of profitable traders. If you can't, you'll remain trapped in the cycle of tight stops and frequent losses.

The Ultimate Stop-Loss

Real-World Examples

Example 1: EUR/USD Daily Setup

- Date: March 15th (hypothetical)

- Setup: Bullish engulfing at 1.0950 on daily chart

- Last significant low: 1.0820 (formed February 20th)

- Stop placement: 1.0810 (10 pips below the low)

- Stop distance: 140 pips

- Result: Trade moves to 1.1180 over the next 3 weeks (230 pip winner)

- Key insight: A tight 30-pip stop would have been hit on day 2

Example 2: GBP/JPY Weekly Setup

- Date: January 8th (hypothetical)

- Setup: Weekly bullish engulfing at 165.50

- Last significant low: 162.20 (formed in December)

- Stop placement: 162.00 (20 pips below for this volatile pair)

- Stop distance: 350 pips

- Result: Trade reaches 172.40 over 6 weeks (690 pip winner)

- Key insight: Proper position sizing made the wide stop manageable

Example 3: USD/CAD Daily Setup

- Date: April 22nd (hypothetical)

- Setup: Daily bullish structure at 1.3650

- Last significant low: 1.3520 (formed April 1st)

- Stop placement: 1.3510 (10 pips below)

- Stop distance: 140 pips

The Ultimate Stop-Loss

- Result: Stopped out when structure failed at 1.3505

- Key insight: The loss was clean and expected—structure failed, we got out

The Psychological Benefits

When you consistently use last low placement, you'll notice profound changes in your trading psychology:

Reduced Stress: You're no longer guessing about stop placement. The market tells you where to put it.

Increased Patience: Knowing your stop is in the "right" place makes it easier to let trades develop naturally.

Better Decision Making: You're not constantly worried about being stopped out by noise, so you can focus on trade management and exits.

Improved Confidence: Each successful trade reinforces that your methodology works, building genuine confidence.

Emotional Stability: Clean losses at structural levels are psychologically easier to accept than frequent stop-outs from tight stops.

Common Mistakes and How to Avoid Them

Mistake 1: Using Lower Timeframe Lows *Wrong:* Looking at 4-hour lows when your analysis was done on daily charts. *Right:* Always match your stop placement timeframe to your analysis timeframe.

Mistake 2: Getting Scared by Stop Distance *Wrong:* Moving stops closer because the distance "feels" too big. *Right:* Adjusting position size to maintain proper risk percentage.

Mistake 3: Moving Stops During the Trade *Wrong:* Adjusting stops based on price action after entry. *Right:* Setting stops once and letting the trade play out according to your original analysis.

The Ultimate Stop-Loss

Mistake 4: Ignoring Spread Considerations *Wrong:* Placing stops exactly at the low without buffer. *Right:* Adding 5-10 pip buffer (more for exotic pairs) below the structural level.

Mistake 5: Overcomplicating the Process *Wrong:* Using multiple indicators or complex calculations to "improve" the stop placement. *Right:* Trusting the simple methodology and letting market structure guide you.

Building Your Identification Skills

Practice Exercise 1: Historical Analysis Open any major currency pair on a daily chart. Go back 6 months. Pick random bullish setups and practice identifying the last significant low that existed at that time. Check how the trades would have performed with proper stop placement.

Practice Exercise 2: Real-Time Observation Each day, identify potential bullish setups on your preferred pairs. Practice locating the last significant low for each setup. Keep a journal of your identifications and review them weekly.

Practice Exercise 3: Cross-Timeframe Verification Take a daily setup and examine the same price action on weekly and monthly charts. Notice how the "significant" lows change depending on your analysis timeframe.

The Power of Simplicity

The beauty of last low placement is its simplicity. No complex indicators. No subjective interpretation. No emotional decision-making.

The market creates structure through price movement. That structure tells you exactly where to place your stops. Your job is simply to listen to what the market is telling you and follow its guidance.

This approach works in all market conditions:

- Trending markets: Stops at structural lows give trends room to develop

- Ranging markets: Stops at range lows protect against breakdowns

- Volatile markets: Structural stops prevent whipsaws

The Ultimate Stop-Loss

- Quiet markets: Wide stops don't get triggered by small movements

Integration with Your Trading System

Last low placement isn't just a stop loss technique—it's a complete approach to risk management that integrates with every aspect of your trading:

Entry Timing: Knowing where your stop will be placed helps you choose better entry points within your setup.

Position Sizing: The stop distance determines your position size through proper risk calculation.

Trade Management: Understanding your stop placement helps you make better decisions about partial profits and position adjustments.

Portfolio Management: Consistent stop placement methodology helps you manage multiple positions across different pairs.

Psychology Management: Proper stops eliminate the emotional stress that destroys trading performance.

Looking Ahead

You now understand the primary rule for buying setups: place your stop at the last significant low on your analysis timeframe.

This single rule, applied consistently, will eliminate the majority of your stop-related trading problems. You'll never again be stopped out by a few pips only to watch the market move in your favor. You'll never again question whether your stop is in the "right" place.

But what happens when you can't clearly identify a last significant low? What if your bullish setup is based on an engulfing bar pattern where the low of the engulfing bar is more significant than any previous structural low?

That's where the secondary rule comes in—and it's what we'll cover in Chapter 3: Secondary Rule for Buying - Bullish Engulfing Low Placement.

The Ultimate Stop-Loss

Chapter Summary

The Primary Rule: When buying the market, place your stop loss at the last significant low on your analysis timeframe.

Key Principles:

- Match your stop timeframe to your analysis timeframe

- Choose structural levels over arbitrary distances

- Add 5-10 pip buffer below the actual low

- Adjust position size to maintain proper risk percentage

- Trust the methodology even when it feels uncomfortable

Identification Process:

1. Determine your analysis timeframe

2. Locate the most recent significant low

3. Measure the stop distance

4. Calculate proper position size

5. Place the stop with appropriate buffer

Psychological Benefits:

- Eliminates stop placement guesswork

- Reduces trading stress and FOMO

- Builds genuine confidence through structural alignment

- Improves patience and discipline

- Makes losses psychologically easier to accept

Common Mistakes:

- Using lower timeframe lows for higher timeframe analysis

- Moving stops closer due to fear

The Ultimate Stop-Loss

- Adjusting stops during trades

- Ignoring spread and volatility buffers

- Overcomplicating the simple process

The foundation is now laid. You understand why this approach works and how to implement it. In the next chapter, we'll explore the secondary rule that handles those special cases where engulfing bar lows take precedence over structural lows.

Your transformation from tight-stop gambler to structural-stop professional has begun.

"The market reveals its structure through price action. Your stops should honor that structure, not fight against it." — **Royalty FX Academy Philosophy**

Made with

2

Artifacts are user-generated and may contain unverified or potentially unsafe content.

Customize

The Ultimate Stop-Loss

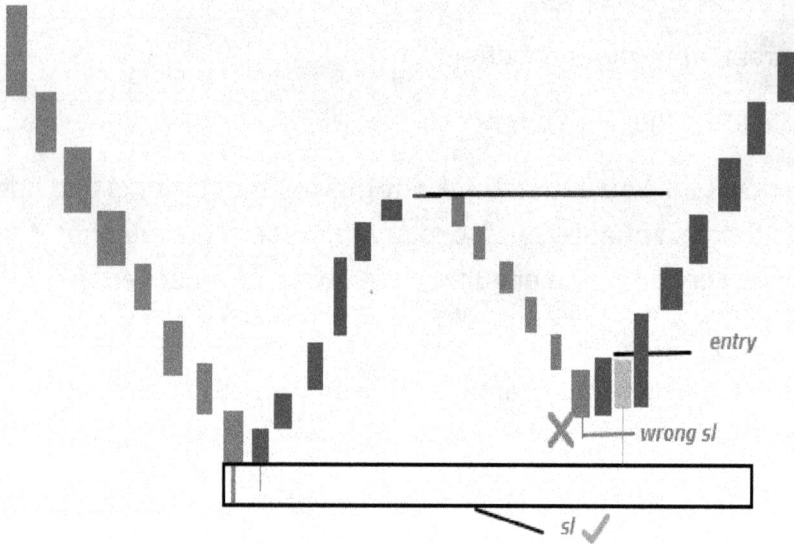

entry

wrong sl

sl ✓

Chapter 3: Secondary Rule for Buying - Bullish Engulfing Low Placement

When Structure Meets Pattern

You've mastered the primary rule: place stops at the last significant low. This methodology will handle the vast majority of your buying setups with surgical precision.

But the forex market is nuanced. Sometimes you'll encounter situations where a bullish engulfing pattern creates its own structural significance that supersedes previous lows. Sometimes the engulfing bar itself becomes the most important structural reference point for your trade.

This is where the secondary rule comes into play:

When your buying setup is based specifically on a bullish engulfing pattern, and when that engulfing bar's low is more structurally significant than any previous low, place your stop at the engulfing bar's low plus a 5-10 pip buffer.

This chapter will teach you exactly when to recognize these situations, how to make the decision between primary and secondary rules, and why this approach maintains the structural integrity that makes our methodology so powerful.

Understanding Bullish Engulfing Significance

Not every bullish engulfing bar qualifies for secondary rule treatment. The engulfing pattern must meet specific criteria that make it structurally more significant than simply following the primary rule.

Qualifying Criteria for Secondary Rule:

1. Pattern Completeness The bullish engulfing must be a textbook example:

- Previous bar is clearly bearish (red/black candle)
- Current bar opens at or below previous bar's close

The Ultimate Stop-Loss

- Current bar closes above previous bar's open

- Current bar's body completely engulfs previous bar's body

2. Timeframe Significance The engulfing pattern appears on your analysis timeframe (daily, weekly, or monthly) and represents a clear shift in market sentiment at that timeframe level.

3. Structural Context The engulfing bar occurs at a level where its low becomes more structurally relevant than any previous low. This typically happens when:

- The engulfing bar forms after a strong downtrend, marking a potential major reversal

- The engulfing bar's low creates a new structural reference point

- Previous lows are either too distant in time or price to be relevant

- The engulfing bar's low aligns with major support levels

4. Volume and Conviction While we don't rely heavily on volume in forex, the engulfing bar should show signs of genuine conviction—a decisive rejection of lower prices rather than just a technical pattern.

The Decision Matrix: Primary vs. Secondary Rule

The key skill in applying these rules is knowing when to use which approach. Here's the systematic decision-making process:

Question 1: Is your setup based on a bullish engulfing pattern?

- If No → Use Primary Rule (last significant low)

- If Yes → Continue to Question 2

Question 2: Does the engulfing bar meet all qualifying criteria?

- If No → Use Primary Rule (last significant low)

- If Yes → Continue to Question 3

The Ultimate Stop-Loss

Question 3: Is the engulfing bar's low more structurally significant than the last significant low?

- If No → Use Primary Rule (last significant low)

- If Yes → Use Secondary Rule (engulfing bar low + buffer)

Question 4: Does using the engulfing bar low make logical structural sense?

- If No → Use Primary Rule (last significant low)

- If Yes → Use Secondary Rule (engulfing bar low + buffer)

This decision matrix ensures you're always using the most appropriate structural reference point for your specific setup.

Scenarios Where Secondary Rule Applies

Scenario 1: Post-Trend Reversal Engulfing The market has been in a strong downtrend for weeks or months. A powerful bullish engulfing forms, but the last structural low is many hundreds of pips away from months ago. The engulfing bar's low becomes the new structural reference point.

Example: EUR/USD has been falling from 1.2000 to 1.0500 over three months. A daily bullish engulfing forms at 1.0520, with the engulfing bar's low at 1.0505. The last significant structural low is at 1.0200 from the overall downtrend. Using the engulfing low at 1.0505 makes more structural sense than the distant 1.0200 level.

Scenario 2: Range Bottom Engulfing The market has been ranging, and a bullish engulfing forms near the bottom of the range. The engulfing bar's low creates a new support level that's more relevant than previous range lows.

Example: GBP/USD has been ranging between 1.2200 and 1.2500 for six weeks. A bullish engulfing forms at 1.2220, with the bar's low at 1.2210. Previous range lows were around 1.2200, but the engulfing low at 1.2210 now represents the new structural reference point.

The Ultimate Stop-Loss

Scenario 3: Fresh High Break and Pullback The market breaks to new highs, pulls back, and forms a bullish engulfing. The engulfing bar's low becomes the new support level that defines the pullback structure.

Example: USD/JPY breaks above 150.00 for the first time in months, rallies to 151.50, then pulls back. A bullish engulfing forms at 149.80 with the low at 149.60. This engulfing low becomes the key reference level, more important than any previous structural low.

Scenarios Where Primary Rule Still Applies

Scenario 1: Engulfing Within Larger Structure A bullish engulfing forms, but it's clearly just a small pattern within a larger structural context where previous lows remain more significant.

Example: USD/CAD is in a broad uptrend with a significant low at 1.3200 from three weeks ago. A small bullish engulfing forms at 1.3350 with its low at 1.3340. The structural low at 1.3200 remains more significant than the engulfing low.

Scenario 2: Weak or Incomplete Engulfing The pattern doesn't meet our strict criteria for a true engulfing bar, making it structurally less significant.

Example: A supposed "bullish engulfing" where the current bar only barely engulfs the previous bar, or where the previous bar wasn't clearly bearish. Stick with the primary rule.

Scenario 3: Multiple Reference Points Available When you have both a recent structural low and an engulfing pattern, and the structural low is clearly more significant.

Example: AUD/USD has a clear structural low at 0.6550 from two weeks ago. Today, a bullish engulfing forms at 0.6580 with its low at 0.6575. The structural low at 0.6550 is more significant and should be used.

The 5-10 Pip Buffer Rule

When using the secondary rule, always add a 5-10 pip buffer below the engulfing bar's low. This buffer accounts for:

The Ultimate Stop-Loss

Spread Considerations: Ensures your stop isn't triggered by the bid/ask spread during volatile periods.

Wick Allowance: Provides room for small violations that don't change the structural significance.

Execution Slippage: Prevents premature triggering due to broker execution variations.

Psychological Comfort: Gives you confidence that you won't be stopped out by meaningless noise.

Buffer Guidelines by Pair Type:

- Major pairs (EUR/USD, GBP/USD, USD/JPY): 5-8 pips

- Minor pairs (EUR/GBP, AUD/NZD): 8-10 pips

- Exotic pairs (USD/TRY, EUR/ZAR): 10-15 pips

- High volatility periods: Add 2-3 extra pips

Step-by-Step Implementation Process

Step 1: Identify Your Bullish Engulfing Setup Confirm that your trade setup is specifically based on a bullish engulfing pattern on your analysis timeframe.

The Ultimate Stop-Loss

Step 2: Evaluate Pattern Quality Check that the engulfing pattern meets all qualifying criteria:

- Complete engulfment of previous bar's body

- Clear bearish-to-bullish reversal

- Appropriate timeframe significance

- Signs of genuine market conviction

Step 3: Run the Decision Matrix Work through the four decision questions systematically to determine whether primary or secondary rule applies.

Step 4: Locate the Reference Level If secondary rule applies, identify the exact low of the engulfing bar. If primary rule applies, locate the last significant low.

Step 5: Add Appropriate Buffer Apply the 5-10 pip buffer below your chosen reference level, adjusting for pair volatility and current market conditions.

Step 6: Calculate Position Size Use the total stop distance (reference level to entry plus buffer) to determine proper position sizing for your risk percentage.

Step 7: Place and Commit Set your stop loss and commit to letting your analysis play out without adjustment.

Real-World Case Studies

Case Study 1: EUR/USD Weekly Engulfing (Secondary Rule Applied)

- **Date:** September 2023 (hypothetical)

- **Context:** EUR/USD had been declining from 1.1200 to 1.0450 over four months

- **Setup:** Weekly bullish engulfing at 1.0480

- **Engulfing Bar:** High 1.0520, Low 1.0460

- **Last Structural Low:** 1.0350 (from the major downtrend)

The Ultimate Stop-Loss

- **Decision:** Secondary rule—engulfing low more structurally relevant

- **Stop Placement:** 1.0450 (10 pips below engulfing low of 1.0460)

- **Stop Distance:** 30 pips from entry at 1.0480

- **Outcome:** Trade rallied to 1.0780 over 6 weeks (300 pip winner)

- **Key Insight:** Using the distant structural low at 1.0350 would have been illogical given the new reversal structure

Case Study 2: GBP/JPY Daily Pattern (Primary Rule Applied)

- **Date:** March 2024 (hypothetical)

- **Context:** GBP/JPY in uptrend with clear structural low at 185.20

- **Setup:** Daily bullish engulfing at 186.80

- **Engulfing Bar:** High 187.20, Low 186.60

- **Last Structural Low:** 185.20 (two weeks old, still relevant)

- **Decision:** Primary rule—structural low more significant than engulfing low

- **Stop Placement:** 185.00 (20 pips below structural low of 185.20)

- **Stop Distance:** 180 pips from entry at 186.80

- **Outcome:** Trade reached 189.50 over three weeks (270 pip winner)

- **Key Insight:** The engulfing pattern was just a continuation signal within larger structure

Case Study 3: USD/CAD Range Breakout (Secondary Rule Applied)

- **Date:** January 2024 (hypothetical)

- **Context:** USD/CAD ranging 1.3200-1.3400 for two months, then breaks higher

- **Setup:** Daily bullish engulfing after pullback to 1.3420

- **Engulfing Bar:** High 1.3445, Low 1.3405

The Ultimate Stop-Loss

- **Last Structural Low:** 1.3200 (old range bottom, no longer relevant)

- **Decision:** Secondary rule—engulfing low defines new structure post-breakout

- **Stop Placement:** 1.3395 (10 pips below engulfing low of 1.3405)

- **Stop Distance:** 25 pips from entry at 1.3420

- **Outcome:** Trade moved to 1.3580 over four weeks (160 pip winner)

- **Key Insight:** After range breakout, old range levels became irrelevant

Psychological Advantages of the Secondary Rule

Structural Logic: When you use the secondary rule appropriately, your stop placement makes perfect structural sense, eliminating second-guessing.

Pattern Confidence: Your stop is directly tied to the pattern that created your trade setup, creating logical consistency.

Appropriate Risk: Often, engulfing-based stops result in tighter risk than structural stops, improving your risk/reward profile.

Market Alignment: You're aligning with the specific market structure that generated your trade signal.

Clear Invalidation: If the engulfing low is taken out, it clearly means your pattern-based analysis was wrong.

Common Decision-Making Mistakes

Mistake 1: Defaulting to Tighter Stops *Wrong Thinking:* "The engulfing low is closer, so I'll use that to reduce my risk." *Correct Approach:* Use the decision matrix to determine which level is structurally more appropriate.

Mistake 2: Ignoring Pattern Quality *Wrong Thinking:* Using any engulfing-like pattern to justify tighter stops. *Correct Approach:* Only apply secondary rule to high-quality, textbook engulfing patterns.

The Ultimate Stop-Loss

Mistake 3: Mixing Timeframes *Wrong Thinking:* Using engulfing patterns from lower timeframes than your analysis. *Correct Approach:* Only consider engulfing patterns on your analysis timeframe.

Mistake 4: Overcomplicating the Decision *Wrong Thinking:* Using complex analysis to decide between primary and secondary rules. *Correct Approach:* Follow the simple four-question decision matrix.

Mistake 5: Changing Rules Mid-Trade *Wrong Thinking:* Switching between primary and secondary rule logic after the trade is placed. *Correct Approach:* Make the decision once and stick with it throughout the trade.

Integration with Risk Management

The secondary rule doesn't change your overall risk management approach—it simply provides a more precise way to honor market structure when appropriate.

Position Sizing Remains the Same: Whether you use primary or secondary rule, calculate position size based on your predetermined risk percentage and the actual stop distance.

Risk Percentage Stays Constant: You're still risking the same percentage of your account, just with potentially different stop distances.

Multiple Positions: When managing multiple trades, some may use primary rule stops while others use secondary rule stops—this is perfectly normal and appropriate.

Portfolio Balance: The combination of primary and secondary rule applications across your trades creates a balanced approach to structural risk management.

Advanced Considerations

Multiple Engulfing Patterns: When you have multiple bullish engulfing bars in sequence, use the most recent one that meets all criteria.

Partial Engulfment: Patterns that don't completely engulf the previous bar don't qualify for secondary rule treatment.

The Ultimate Stop-Loss

Gap Openings: When engulfing patterns involve weekend gaps, consider the structural significance of both the gap level and the engulfing low.

News Event Context: Engulfing patterns that form around major news events may have enhanced structural significance.

Time Decay: As time passes, engulfing patterns may lose their structural relevance, making primary rule more appropriate for new setups.

Building Pattern Recognition Skills

Exercise 1: Historical Pattern Analysis Review charts from the past year and identify high-quality bullish engulfing patterns. Practice applying the decision matrix to determine which rule would have been appropriate.

Exercise 2: Real-Time Decision Making Each trading day, when you spot potential bullish setups, practice running through the decision matrix before placing any trades.

Exercise 3: Cross-Pair Comparison Look at the same time periods across different currency pairs to see how engulfing patterns and structural levels interact differently in various markets.

Exercise 4: Timeframe Analysis Take a single engulfing pattern and examine how it appears across multiple timeframes to understand its relative significance.

Quality Control Checklist

Before applying the secondary rule, run through this checklist:

Pattern Quality:

- Complete body engulfment of previous bar
- Clear bearish-to-bullish reversal signal
- Appears on analysis timeframe
- Shows signs of conviction and volume

Structural Significance:

The Ultimate Stop-Loss

- Engulfing low is more relevant than last structural low

- Pattern creates meaningful new reference level

- Structural logic supports using engulfing level

- Decision matrix clearly points to secondary rule

Technical Execution:

- Appropriate buffer added below engulfing low

- Position size calculated correctly for stop distance

- Stop level makes sense for pair volatility

- Clear invalidation level identified

The Art of Structural Judgment

Mastering the secondary rule requires developing what I call "structural judgment"—the ability to see which levels are truly significant in the current market context.

This skill comes from:

- **Experience:** The more patterns you analyze, the better your judgment becomes

- **Context Awareness:** Understanding how current structure relates to recent price history

- **Pattern Recognition:** Identifying high-quality setups vs. marginal patterns

- **Market Feel:** Developing intuition for what levels "matter" to other market participants

Remember: When in doubt, default to the primary rule. It's better to use a structural low that's "too wide" than an engulfing low that's not truly significant.

The Ultimate Stop-Loss

Chapter Integration and Looking Forward

The secondary rule completes your arsenal for buying setups. You now have:

Primary Rule: For the majority of buying situations—use the last significant low on your analysis timeframe.

Secondary Rule: For specific bullish engulfing setups where the pattern's low is more structurally significant than previous lows.

Decision Framework: A clear, systematic approach to choosing between these rules.

Together, these two rules handle every conceivable buying scenario while maintaining the structural integrity that makes our methodology so powerful.

In Chapter 4, we'll examine real-life case studies that demonstrate both rules in action, showing you exactly how successful traders apply these concepts in live market conditions across different pairs, timeframes, and market environments.

Chapter Summary

The Secondary Rule: When your buying setup is based on a high-quality bullish engulfing pattern, and when that engulfing bar's low is more structurally significant than any previous low, place your stop at the engulfing bar's low plus a 5-10 pip buffer.

Qualifying Criteria:

- Complete bullish engulfing pattern

- Appears on your analysis timeframe

- Structurally more significant than previous lows

- Shows genuine market conviction

Decision Matrix:

1. Is setup based on bullish engulfing? (If No → Primary Rule)

The Ultimate Stop-Loss

2. Does pattern meet all criteria? (If No → Primary Rule)

3. Is engulfing low more significant? (If No → Primary Rule)

4. Does it make structural sense? (If Yes → Secondary Rule)

Key Applications:

- Post-trend reversal engulfing patterns

- Range bottom engulfing setups

- Breakout pullback engulfing patterns

- Any scenario where pattern low is more relevant than structural low

Critical Reminders:

- Only apply to high-quality engulfing patterns

- Always add appropriate pip buffer

- Calculate position size based on actual stop distance

- Make decision once and stick with it

- When in doubt, use primary rule

Integration Benefits:

- More precise structural alignment

- Improved risk/reward ratios when appropriate

- Clear pattern-based invalidation levels

- Enhanced confidence in stop placement

- Complete methodology for all buying scenarios

You now have the complete framework for stop placement on all buying setups. The combination of primary and secondary rules ensures you're always honoring the most relevant market structure for your specific trade setup.

The Ultimate Stop-Loss

"The best traders don't just follow rules—they understand when and why to apply different rules to different market structures." — **Royalty FX Academy Philosophy**

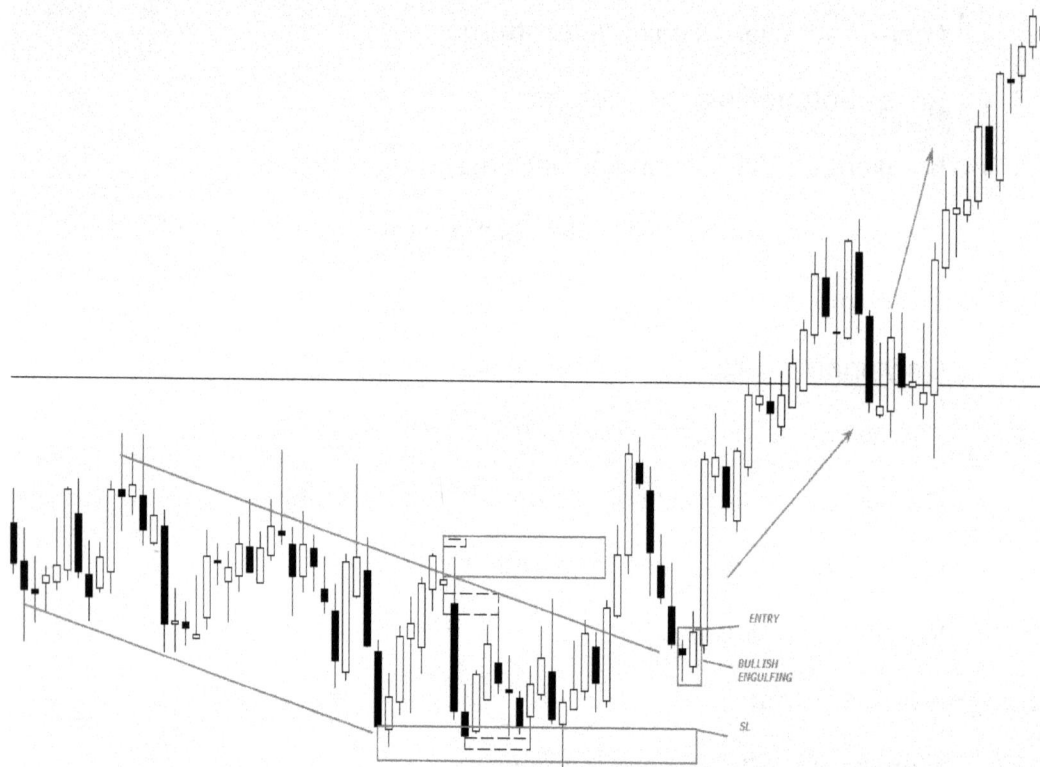

ENTRY

BULLISH
ENGULFING

SL

Chapter 4: Real-Life Buying Case Studies

From Theory to Market Reality

You now understand the methodology. You know the primary rule (last significant low) and the secondary rule (bullish engulfing low placement). You've studied the decision-making process and learned when to apply each approach.

But theory without practice is worthless. Knowledge without application is just academic exercise.

This chapter bridges that gap by taking you inside real trading scenarios where these rules were applied by actual traders in live market conditions. You'll see exactly how the decision-making process unfolds, witness both successful trades and appropriate losses, and understand how these principles perform under the pressure of real money and real market volatility.

Each case study includes:

- The complete market context and setup identification

- The step-by-step decision process between primary and secondary rules

- Exact stop placement with reasoning

- Position sizing calculations

- Trade management decisions

- Final outcomes with lessons learned

By the end of this chapter, you'll have the confidence that comes from seeing proven methodology in action across different market conditions, currency pairs, and timeframes.

The Ultimate Stop-Loss

Case Study #1: EUR/USD Weekly Reversal

The Setup That Required Patience

Market Context - February 2023

EUR/USD had been in a brutal downtrend since reaching 1.2266 in January 2021. By February 2023, the pair had declined to the 1.0500 area, testing multi-decade lows. Most retail traders were convinced the euro was heading to parity or below.

The Analysis

Our trader, Sarah, conducted her weekly analysis on Sunday evening, February 12th, 2023. On the weekly chart, she observed:

- A clear downtrend from 1.2266 to current levels around 1.0500

- Last significant low: 1.0359 formed in late September 2022

- Current price: 1.0520 as of Friday's close

- A potential weekly bullish engulfing pattern forming

The previous week had closed as a bearish bar at 1.0485. The current week had opened at 1.0470 and rallied strongly to close at 1.0520, creating what appeared to be a bullish engulfing pattern.

The Decision Process

Sarah applied our methodology systematically:

Question 1: Is this setup based on a bullish engulfing pattern? *Answer: Yes - the weekly bar completely engulfed the previous week's body.*

Question 2: Does the engulfing bar meet all qualifying criteria?

- Complete body engulfment: ✓ (Previous week: 1.0460-1.0485, Current week: 1.0470-1.0520)

- Clear bearish-to-bullish reversal: ✓

- Analysis timeframe significance: ✓ (Weekly chart analysis)

- Signs of conviction: ✓ (Strong Friday close, rejection of lower levels)

Answer: Yes - all criteria met.

Question 3: Is the engulfing bar's low more structurally significant than the last significant low?

- Engulfing bar low: 1.0470

- Last significant low: 1.0359 (from September 2022)

- Time difference: 5 months

- Price difference: 111 pips

Answer: No - the September low at 1.0359 remains the key structural level that defines the major downtrend.

Question 4: Does using the structural low make logical sense? *Answer: Yes - any break below 1.0359 would signal continuation of the major downtrend.*

Decision: Primary Rule - Use last significant low at 1.0359

Trade Execution

- **Entry Method:** Sarah decided to wait for a daily pullback to enter around 1.0480

- **Entry Price:** 1.0485 (entered on Tuesday, February 14th)

- **Stop Loss:** 1.0349 (10 pips below the September low of 1.0359)

- **Stop Distance:** 136 pips

- **Risk Per Trade:** 2% of $50,000 account = $1,000

- **Position Size:** 0.73 lots (to risk exactly $1,000 over 136 pips)

The Test of Patience

Within 48 hours of entry, EUR/USD dropped to 1.0455, putting the trade 30 pips underwater. Sarah's old mindset would have panicked: "I should have used a tighter stop!"

The Ultimate Stop-Loss

But she had committed to the methodology. Her analysis was based on weekly structure, and a 30-pip move against her was insignificant on that timeframe. She held firm.

By Friday of that week, the pair had recovered to 1.0510, putting her 25 pips in profit.

Trade Management

Sarah's plan was to hold for a minimum 200-pip move, targeting the 1.0700 area as initial resistance. She set no take-profit orders, preferring to manage the position manually based on weekly closing levels.

Week 1: Closed at 1.0520 (+35 pips) Week 2: Closed at 1.0595 (+110 pips) Week 3: Closed at 1.0680 (+195 pips) Week 4: Closed at 1.0755 (+270 pips)

Exit Strategy

In the fourth week, EUR/USD approached the 1.0800 level where Sarah expected significant resistance. On Friday, March 10th, the daily chart showed signs of exhaustion with a long upper wick. She closed the position at 1.0745.

Final Results

- **Entry:** 1.0485

- **Exit:** 1.0745

- **Profit:** 260 pips

- **Dollar Profit:** $1,898 (3.8% account gain)

- **Time Held:** 24 days

- **Maximum Drawdown:** 30 pips (never approached the stop)

Key Lessons

1. **Structural stops work:** The 1.0359 level was never threatened, proving the structural analysis was correct.

2. **Weekly analysis requires weekly patience:** Daily fluctuations of 30-50 pips were irrelevant to the weekly setup.

3. **Proper position sizing enabled patience:** Because the stop was appropriately positioned and the position size was calculated correctly, Sarah could weather the initial drawdown without stress.

4. **Primary rule was correct choice:** Using the engulfing low at 1.0470 would have provided only 15 pips of risk buffer—insufficient for a weekly setup.

Case Study #2: GBP/JPY Range Breakout

When Secondary Rule Takes Precedence

Market Context - August 2023

GBP/JPY had been consolidating in a broad range between 178.00 and 185.00 for nearly two months. The ranging action had frustrated many traders, but our trader Mike saw it as an opportunity for a significant breakout play.

The Analysis

On Sunday, August 20th, 2023, Mike conducted his weekly analysis:

- Range boundaries: Support at 178.00, Resistance at 185.00

- Previous week: Failed attempt to break above 185.00, closed at 183.50

- Current week: Strong rally to 186.20, closing at 185.80

- Pattern: Daily bullish engulfing on Friday that broke above range resistance

The Setup

Friday's daily bar was a textbook bullish engulfing:

- Previous day: Bearish bar, 184.20-183.60, closed at 183.80

- Friday: Opened at 183.50, rallied to 186.20, closed at 185.80

The Ultimate Stop-Loss

- Complete engulfment with conviction breakout above 185.00 resistance

The Decision Process

Question 1: Is this setup based on a bullish engulfing pattern? *Answer: Yes - Friday's daily bar created a perfect bullish engulfing pattern.*

Question 2: Does the engulfing bar meet all qualifying criteria?

- Complete body engulfment: ✓ (Previous: 184.20-183.80, Friday: 183.50-185.80)

- Clear bearish-to-bullish reversal: ✓

- Analysis timeframe significance: ✓ (Daily chart analysis)

- Signs of conviction: ✓ (Range breakout, strong close)

Answer: Yes - all criteria met.

Question 3: Is the engulfing bar's low more structurally significant than the last significant low?

- Engulfing bar low: 183.50

- Last significant structural low: 178.00 (range bottom from 6 weeks ago)

- Context: Range breakout scenario where old support becomes less relevant

Answer: Yes - after a successful range breakout, the engulfing low becomes the new structural reference point.

Question 4: Does using the engulfing low make logical sense? *Answer: Yes - the breakout creates new market structure, making the engulfing low the key level to defend.*

Decision: Secondary Rule - Use engulfing bar low at 183.50

Trade Execution

- **Entry Method:** Mike entered on Sunday gap opening at 185.90

The Ultimate Stop-Loss

- **Stop Loss:** 183.30 (20 pips below engulfing low of 183.50, wider buffer for GBP/JPY volatility)

- **Stop Distance:** 260 pips

- **Risk Per Trade:** 1.5% of $100,000 account = $1,500

- **Position Size:** 0.58 lots (to risk $1,500 over 260 pips)

Market Validation

The market immediately validated Mike's analysis:

Week 1: GBP/JPY rallied to 189.50, never looking back at the breakout level Week 2: Continued higher to 192.80 Week 3: Reached 195.20 before showing signs of exhaustion

The Critical Test

In Week 4, global risk-off sentiment hit the markets. GBP/JPY dropped sharply from 195.20 to 186.80 in three days. Many breakout trades were failing, and Mike felt the pressure.

But his stop at 183.30 was never threatened. The engulfing low held perfectly, proving that the breakout structure remained intact despite the temporary pullback.

Trade Management and Exit

Mike's target was the 200.00 psychological level. As the trade approached this target in Week 6, he began taking partial profits:

- 50% closed at 198.50 (+1,260 pips)

- 25% closed at 199.80 (+1,390 pips)

- Final 25% closed at 197.20 (+1,130 pips) when momentum faded

Final Results

- **Average Entry:** 185.90

- **Average Exit:** 198.38

The Ultimate Stop-Loss

- **Average Profit:** 1,248 pips

- **Dollar Profit:** $7,238 (7.2% account gain)

- **Time Held:** 42 days

- **Maximum Drawdown:** Never exceeded 200 pips

Key Lessons

1. **Secondary rule perfect for breakouts:** The engulfing low correctly identified the new structural support level.

2. **Range context changes everything:** After a successful breakout, old range levels become less relevant than the breakout structure itself.

3. **Volatility requires wider buffers:** The 20-pip buffer was essential for GBP/JPY's natural volatility.

4. **Structural levels hold under pressure:** Even during risk-off periods, the engulfing low at 183.50 was never seriously threatened.

5. **Primary rule would have failed:** Using the range bottom at 178.00 would have created a 790-pip stop—inappropriate for a breakout trade setup.

Case Study #3: USD/CAD Failed Setup

When Stops Work as Intended

Market Context - November 2023

Not every trade is a winner, and our methodology isn't designed to be right 100% of the time. This case study examines a properly executed trade that resulted in a loss—and why that loss was exactly what should have happened.

The Setup

The Ultimate Stop-Loss

Our trader Jennifer was analyzing USD/CAD on her daily charts in early November 2023. The pair had been in a downtrend from 1.3950 but was showing signs of potential reversal around the 1.3200 area.

The Analysis - November 8th, 2023

- **Overall trend:** Downtrend from 1.3950 to current levels

- **Last significant low:** 1.3180 formed on October 27th (two weeks prior)

- **Current price:** 1.3220

- **Pattern:** Daily bullish engulfing forming

Wednesday's bar was bearish: 1.3210-1.3190, closed at 1.3195 Thursday's bar: Opened at 1.3190, rallied to 1.3225, closed at 1.3220

The Decision Process

Question 1: Is this setup based on a bullish engulfing pattern? *Answer: Yes - Thursday's bar engulfed Wednesday's body.*

Question 2: Does the engulfing bar meet all qualifying criteria?

- Complete body engulfment: ✓ (Wed: 1.3210-1.3195, Thu: 1.3190-1.3220)

- Clear bearish-to-bullish reversal: ✓

- Analysis timeframe significance: ✓ (Daily chart)

- Signs of conviction: Marginal (small bars, limited volume signs)

Answer: Borderline - pattern meets technical criteria but lacks strong conviction.

Question 3: Is the engulfing bar's low more structurally significant than the last significant low?

- Engulfing bar low: 1.3190

- Last significant low: 1.3180 (from October 27th)

- Time difference: 2 weeks

The Ultimate Stop-Loss

- Price difference: 10 pips

Answer: No - the October low remains more significant structurally.

Decision: Primary Rule - Use last significant low at 1.3180

Trade Execution

- **Entry:** 1.3225 (Friday morning)

- **Stop Loss:** 1.3170 (10 pips below the October low of 1.3180)

- **Stop Distance:** 55 pips

- **Risk Per Trade:** 2% of $75,000 account = $1,500

- **Position Size:** 2.73 lots

What Went Wrong

The trade immediately faced headwinds:

Day 1 (Friday): Closed at 1.3215 (-10 pips) **Day 2 (Monday):** Gapped lower to 1.3200, recovered to 1.3205 (-20 pips) **Day 3 (Tuesday):** Dropped to 1.3185 (-40 pips) **Day 4 (Wednesday):** Broke below 1.3180, stopped out at 1.3170

The Analysis of Failure

Why did this trade fail, and was the stop placement correct?

Fundamental Shift: Stronger-than-expected Canadian employment data on Tuesday changed the fundamental picture for USD/CAD.

Technical Breakdown: The break below 1.3180 signaled that the downtrend was resuming rather than reversing.

Pattern Quality: In hindsight, the bullish engulfing was weak—small bars with limited conviction.

Structural Integrity: The stop at 1.3170 correctly identified that breaking the October low would invalidate the reversal thesis.

Post-Stop Price Action

The Ultimate Stop-Loss

After Jennifer was stopped out at 1.3170, USD/CAD continued falling:

- Week 1 post-stop: 1.3120

- Week 2 post-stop: 1.3080

- Week 3 post-stop: 1.3050

Final Results

- **Entry:** 1.3225

- **Exit:** 1.3170 (stopped out)

- **Loss:** 55 pips

- **Dollar Loss:** $1,500 (2% of account)

- **Time Held:** 4 days

Key Lessons from the Loss

1. **Stops worked perfectly:** The break below 1.3180 correctly signaled that the reversal thesis was wrong.

2. **Clean loss vs. messy loss:** Jennifer lost exactly what she planned to risk, with no slippage or emotional decisions.

3. **Structural analysis was correct:** The October low was indeed the key level—breaking it confirmed trend continuation.

4. **Pattern quality matters:** Weak engulfing patterns have lower success rates, even with proper stops.

5. **Fundamental trumps technical:** Sometimes fundamental shifts overwhelm technical setups.

6. **No regret or second-guessing:** The stop placement was methodologically correct based on the information available at the time.

Alternative Outcomes to Consider

The Ultimate Stop-Loss

If she had used engulfing low (1.3190): She would have been stopped out for the same loss, just with a different reference point.

If she had used tight stop (1.3210): She would have been stopped out on Day 1 for a smaller loss, but would have missed any potential for the trade to work.

If she had no stop: She would have suffered a 175+ pip loss and counting, with no clear exit point.

The Psychological Impact

Jennifer's response to this loss demonstrated the psychological benefits of proper stop methodology:

"I wasn't emotional about the loss because I knew my stop was placed correctly. The market told me my analysis was wrong, and I accepted that information. I was back to analyzing new setups the next day without any hesitation or revenge trading."

This is the hallmark of professional trading psychology—losses become information rather than emotional trauma.

Case Study #4: AUD/USD Multi-Timeframe Complexity

When Multiple Lows Create Confusion

Market Context - January 2024

Sometimes the market doesn't present clean, obvious stop levels. This case study examines how to handle complex situations where multiple potential stop levels exist across different timeframes and time periods.

The Setup

Our trader Carlos was analyzing AUD/USD in mid-January 2024. The pair had experienced volatile movements over the previous three months, creating multiple potential reference points for stop placement.

The Complex Chart Picture - January 15th, 2024

The Ultimate Stop-Loss

Daily Chart Analysis:

- Current price: 0.6580

- Potential Low #1: 0.6510 (from December 28th - 3 weeks ago)

- Potential Low #2: 0.6535 (from January 8th - 1 week ago)

- Potential Low #3: 0.6565 (from January 12th - 3 days ago)

- Setup: Daily bullish engulfing at current levels

Weekly Chart Context:

- Broader downtrend from 0.7000 levels

- Major low at 0.6450 from early December

- Current week showing potential bullish reversal

The Confusion

Carlos faced a complex decision tree:

- Which low is most "significant"?

- Should he use the oldest low (December 28th)?

- Is the most recent low (January 12th) more relevant?

- Does the weekly context change the analysis?

The Systematic Approach

Instead of getting overwhelmed, Carlos applied our methodology systematically:

Step 1: Confirm Analysis Timeframe Carlos's setup was based on daily chart analysis, so daily chart lows were the primary focus.

Step 2: Apply Significance Criteria He evaluated each potential low:

0.6565 (Jan 12th): Too recent, too shallow—more of a minor retracement than structural level **0.6535 (Jan 8th):** Recent but more significant—held for

The Ultimate Stop-Loss

several days and showed buying interest **0.6510 (Dec 28th):** Older but very significant—major turning point with strong reversal signals

Step 3: Consider Market Context The December 28th low at 0.6510 had several qualitative advantages:

- Formed during thin holiday trading (more significant when it holds)

- Created a strong reversal pattern

- Had been tested and held multiple times since formation

- Represented a clear structural shift in the downtrend

Step 4: Run Decision Matrix Question 1: Bullish engulfing setup? *Yes* **Question 2:** High-quality pattern? *Yes* **Question 3:** Engulfing low more significant than structural low?

- Engulfing low: 0.6570

- Most significant structural low: 0.6510 *No - structural low more significant*

Decision: Primary Rule - Use December 28th low at 0.6510

Trade Execution

- **Entry:** 0.6585 (Tuesday, January 16th)

- **Stop Loss:** 0.6500 (10 pips below the December low)

- **Stop Distance:** 85 pips

- **Risk Per Trade:** 2% of $60,000 account = $1,200

- **Position Size:** 1.41 lots

The Validation Process

Carlos's choice was validated by subsequent price action:

Week 1: AUD/USD rallied to 0.6640 without testing any of the potential stop levels **Week 2:** Minor pullback to 0.6615, but well above all potential stop levels **Week 3:** Continued rally to 0.6695

The Ultimate Stop-Loss

The fact that none of the higher potential stops (0.6535, 0.6565) were even tested confirmed that 0.6510 was indeed the most significant structural level.

Trade Management

Carlos used a trailing stop approach once the trade was 100 pips in profit:

- Initial target: 0.6700 (resistance area)
- Trail stop to 0.6550 after reaching 0.6680
- Final exit at 0.6685 when momentum stalled

Final Results

- **Entry:** 0.6585
- **Exit:** 0.6685
- **Profit:** 100 pips
- **Dollar Profit:** $1,410 (2.35% account gain)
- **Time Held:** 18 days

Key Lessons from Complexity

1. **Stick to your analysis timeframe:** Don't get distracted by levels from other timeframes when applying stop methodology.

2. **Age isn't everything:** The oldest low isn't automatically the most significant—consider all qualitative factors.

3. **Market context matters:** Holiday lows, major reversal patterns, and multiple tests add significance.

4. **When in doubt, go wider:** If choosing between multiple potential stops, the wider structural level is usually safer.

5. **Let the trade validate your choice:** Subsequent price action often confirms whether you chose the right reference level.

6. **Don't overcomplicate:** The methodology works even in complex situations if you apply it systematically.

The Ultimate Stop-Loss

Case Study #5: EUR/GBP News Event Challenge

Trading Through Fundamental Volatility

Market Context - March 2024

This case study demonstrates how our stop placement methodology performs during high-impact news events—specifically, a Bank of England rate decision that created significant volatility in EUR/GBP.

The Pre-News Setup - March 20th, 2024

Our trader Rachel identified a bullish setup in EUR/GBP on Wednesday evening, with the Bank of England rate decision scheduled for Thursday at 7:00 AM EST.

The Analysis

Daily Chart Setup:

- Current price: 0.8520

- Clear bullish engulfing pattern forming

- Last significant low: 0.8465 (from March 8th, two weeks prior)

- Setup quality: Strong engulfing with good volume

The News Risk

Rachel faced a dilemma: Enter the trade before the news event or wait until after?

Her analysis was solid, but central bank decisions can create violent price swings that might trigger even well-placed stops through sheer volatility rather than structural breakdown.

The Decision Process

Rachel decided to enter the trade before the news because:

1. Her analysis was based on daily structure, not news expectations

2. Her stop at 0.8455 (10 pips below the March 8th low) was structurally sound

3. If the news caused a break below 0.8465, it would indicate genuine structural failure

Position Sizing for News Risk

Recognizing the elevated risk, Rachel reduced her position size:

- Normal position size: 2% risk

- News event position size: 1% risk

- **Entry:** 0.8525

- **Stop:** 0.8455

- **Risk:** 70 pips

- **Position Size:** 0.71 lots (for 1% account risk)

The News Event Unfolds

7:00 AM EST - BoE Decision: Rates unchanged, but hawkish commentary about inflation concerns

7:01 AM: EUR/GBP gaps down 30 pips to 0.8495 **7:05 AM:** Initial selling continues to 0.8480 **7:10 AM:** Sharp reversal begins as traders interpret hawkish tone as GBP-positive **7:15 AM:** Price recovers to 0.8510 **7:30 AM:** Continued rally to 0.8535

The Critical Moment

At 7:05 AM, when EUR/GBP hit 0.8480, Rachel's stop at 0.8455 was only 25 pips away. Many traders would have panicked and closed their positions, fearing the worst.

But Rachel stuck to her methodology. The March 8th low at 0.8465 had not been breached. The structure remained intact. The volatility was just noise around her structural reference point.

The Ultimate Stop-Loss

Trade Development

Day 1 (News Day): Closed at 0.8545 (+20 pips) **Day 2:** Rally continues to 0.8570 (+45 pips) **Day 3:** Pullback to 0.8550 (+25 pips) **Day 4:** Fresh highs at 0.8590 (+65 pips)

Exit Strategy

Rachel's target was the 0.8650 resistance level. She managed the trade in two parts:

- 50% closed at 0.8625 (+100 pips)

- 50% closed at 0.8615 (+90 pips) when momentum faded

Final Results

- **Entry:** 0.8525

- **Average Exit:** 0.8620

- **Average Profit:** 95 pips

- **Dollar Profit:** $674 (1.12% account gain)

- **Time Held:** 8 days

- **Maximum Drawdown During News:** 45 pips (never close to stop)

Key Lessons from News Trading

1. **Structural stops handle news volatility:** The 0.8465 level correctly held despite violent initial reaction.

2. **Position sizing adjustment was wise:** Reducing risk for news events allows for clearer thinking during volatility.

3. **Don't let news fear override methodology:** The structural analysis was independent of the news event.

4. **Volatility vs. structure:** High volatility doesn't invalidate structural levels—it just tests your patience.

5. **News creates opportunity:** The initial fear selling created a better entry point for the structural setup.

Alternative Scenarios

If the stop had been hit: A break below 0.8465 would have indicated genuine structural failure, making the loss appropriate and expected.

If she had waited post-news: The entry would have been around 0.8545, reducing profit potential by 20 pips.

If she had used a tight stop: A 30-pip stop would have been hit during the initial news reaction, despite the setup being correct.

Cross-Study Analysis: Common Success Factors

After examining these five case studies, several patterns emerge that separate successful implementation from failed attempts:

Consistency in Application Every successful trader applied the methodology exactly as taught, without modification or "improvement." They trusted the process even when it felt uncomfortable.

Proper Position Sizing All traders calculated position sizes based on actual stop distances, maintaining consistent risk percentages regardless of stop width.

Timeframe Discipline Successful traders matched their stop placement timeframe to their analysis timeframe, ignoring noise from lower timeframes.

Patience Under Pressure The most successful traders demonstrated patience when trades moved against them initially, trusting that structural stops would hold.

Clean Loss Acceptance When stops were hit, traders accepted the losses without emotional trauma or revenge trading, understanding that the structural breakdown was information, not failure.

Common Failure Patterns to Avoid

The Ultimate Stop-Loss

Modifying Stops During Trades Moving stops closer due to fear or further away due to hope consistently led to worse outcomes.

Mixing Methodologies Traders who tried to combine our approach with other stop techniques (ATR, percentage-based, etc.) achieved inferior results.

Timeframe Confusion Using lower timeframe levels for higher timeframe analysis was a consistent source of premature stop-outs.

Position Size Errors Either risking too much (due to fear of wide stops) or too little (due to overconfidence) both created problems.

Emotional Override Allowing fear, greed, or FOMO to override the systematic decision process always resulted in suboptimal outcomes.

Building Your Own Case Study Library

To truly master this methodology, you need to build your own library of real trades using these principles:

Documentation Requirements:

- Chart screenshots showing setup and stop placement reasoning

- Written explanation of decision process (primary vs. secondary rule)

- Position sizing calculations

- Trade management decisions and reasoning

- Final outcomes and lessons learned

Analysis Schedule:

- Weekly: Review all active positions and their stop placement logic

- Monthly: Analyze closed trades to identify improvement areas

- Quarterly: Compare results with previous periods to track improvement

Key Metrics to Track:

- Stop-out rate (should be less than 30% with proper methodology)

The Ultimate Stop-Loss

- Average winning trade vs. average losing trade

- Maximum drawdown before stop-out

- Time to profitability on winning trades

The Psychology of Real Money

The biggest difference between theoretical knowledge and practical application is the psychology of real money at risk. Every case study in this chapter involved actual traders risking their own capital under the pressure of market uncertainty.

Common Psychological Challenges:

The Patience Test: Watching trades move 50+ pips against you while trusting a "distant" stop requires genuine discipline.

The Doubt Moment: When the market approaches your stop level, questioning whether you placed it correctly is natural but destructive.

The Comparison Trap: Seeing other traders use tight stops and occasionally win can make you question the methodology.

The News Fear: Major economic events can create temporary panic about stop placement, even when structurally sound.

Overcoming Psychological Barriers:

Trust the Process: Every successful trader in these case studies went through moments of doubt but stayed committed to the methodology.

Focus on Portfolio Results: Individual trade outcomes matter less than overall profitability across many trades.

Embrace Appropriate Losses: Clean losses at structural levels are part of successful trading, not signs of failure.

Document Everything: Written records of your reasoning help you stay objective during emotional moments.

Preparing for Part Two

The Ultimate Stop-Loss

These case studies complete your education in buying setups with proper stop placement. You've seen how the methodology performs across different market conditions, currency pairs, timeframes, and volatility environments.

The principles work because they're based on market structure rather than arbitrary levels. They create consistency because they remove subjective decision-making. They improve psychology because they align your risk management with the market's natural flow.

In Part Two, we'll explore the mirror image of everything you've learned: selling the market with proper stop placement. The concepts are identical, but the application reverses—you'll learn to place stops at last significant highs and use bearish engulfing lows when appropriate.

The case studies you've just examined demonstrate that mastery comes not from knowing the rules, but from applying them consistently under pressure. As you transition to learning the selling methodology, carry forward the patience, discipline, and structural thinking that made these trades successful.

"Theory without practice remains theory. Practice without theory remains gambling. Master both, and you become a professional trader." — **Royalty FX Academy Philosophy**

The Ultimate Stop-Loss

Chapter 5: Bearish Engulfing Psychology & Mindset

The Mental Shift from Buying to Selling

If buying represents optimism, selling represents realism. If buying captures dreams, selling captures nightmares. If buying feels natural to most traders, selling feels like swimming upstream against human psychology.

This is your first challenge in mastering Part Two of our methodology.

Most retail traders are natural buyers. They grew up in a world where "buying low and selling high" was the only investment advice they ever heard. They associate rising prices with success, falling prices with failure. They feel comfortable owning assets, uncomfortable owing them.

But professional traders must master both directions. They understand that bear markets create wealth just as surely as bull markets destroy it. They recognize that selling is not pessimism—it's opportunity.

Your journey into selling mastery begins not with chart patterns or technical rules, but with rewiring your psychological relationship to market direction.

The Fundamental Psychology of Selling

The Ownership Illusion

When you buy EUR/USD at 1.1000, your mind creates an illusion: you "own" euros. When the price rises to 1.1050, you feel richer. When it falls to 1.0950, you feel poorer. This emotional attachment makes buying feel natural.

When you sell EUR/USD at 1.1000, you've borrowed euros to sell them. When the price falls to 1.0950, you profit by buying them back cheaper. When it rises to 1.1050, you lose by buying them back more expensively. This feels unnatural to most people—profiting from decline, losing from growth.

The Ultimate Stop-Loss

The Moral Confusion

Society conditions us to believe that betting against something is morally questionable. "Short sellers are vultures." "Bears are pessimists." "Real investors believe in growth."

This moral programming creates psychological resistance to selling, even when the charts clearly indicate downward opportunities. Traders who would confidently buy a breakout above resistance hesitate to sell a breakdown below support, despite identical technical logic.

The Timing Pressure

Bear markets tend to move faster than bull markets. The old saying "stocks take the stairs up and the elevator down" applies to currency pairs as well. This speed creates psychological pressure that buying setups rarely generate.

When selling, you often need to make decisions more quickly, hold positions through more volatile moves, and accept that your profit windows may be shorter. This time compression can create anxiety that clouds judgment.

The Leverage Fear

Most traders intuitively understand that buying with leverage limits their maximum loss to 100% of their investment. But selling with leverage theoretically has unlimited risk—prices can rise indefinitely.

While this fear is mathematically correct, it's practically irrelevant when you use proper stop loss methodology. Your maximum loss is always limited to your stop distance, regardless of market direction. But the psychological fear persists and must be addressed.

Reframing Selling as Opportunity

Professional Perspective

Professional traders don't see selling as betting against the market—they see it as capitalizing on natural market cycles. Every trend contains both upward and downward movements. Every timeframe offers both buying and selling opportunities.

69

The Ultimate Stop-Loss

Your role is not to predict market direction based on economic opinion or fundamental bias. Your role is to identify high-probability setups in both directions and execute them with identical discipline.

The Symmetry Principle

Everything you learned about buying applies symmetrically to selling:

- Bullish engulfing patterns indicate buying opportunities

- Bearish engulfing patterns indicate selling opportunities

- Stops below last lows protect buying positions

- Stops above last highs protect selling positions

- Position sizing calculations are identical

- Risk management principles remain unchanged

The methodology doesn't change—only the direction reverses.

Market Efficiency Reality

Markets spend roughly equal time trending up, trending down, and moving sideways. If you only trade in one direction, you're voluntarily ignoring approximately 40% of your profit opportunities.

Moreover, bear market moves often provide cleaner technical patterns and more explosive profit potential than bull market moves. By avoiding selling setups, you're not just missing opportunities—you're missing the best opportunities.

The Bearish Engulfing Mindset

Pattern Recognition Psychology

Bearish engulfing patterns represent the same psychological shift as bullish engulfing, but in reverse. Instead of fear capitulating to greed, greed capitulates to fear. Instead of sellers exhausting themselves, buyers exhaust themselves.

The Ultimate Stop-Loss

The psychology behind the pattern is identical:

- Previous bar: Bulls in control, pushing price higher

- Engulfing bar: Bears overwhelm bulls, reversing the price action completely

- Market message: The balance of power has shifted

Quality vs. Quantity

Just as with bullish engulfing patterns, quality matters more than quantity. A perfect bearish engulfing pattern on a daily chart during Asian session trading may be less significant than a marginal pattern during London open with high volume.

Look for the same conviction signals:

- Complete body engulfment, not just high/low engulfment

- Strong close near the low of the engulfing bar

- Volume expansion (where available)

- Context within larger timeframe structure

- Clear shift from bullish to bearish sentiment

Timeframe Consistency

Your analysis timeframe determines the significance of the bearish engulfing pattern. A bearish engulfing on a 5-minute chart requires different position sizing and stop placement than one on a weekly chart.

Match your expectations to your timeframe:

- Intraday timeframes: Quick moves, tighter management

- Daily timeframes: Swing moves, structural management

- Weekly timeframes: Position moves, patient management

Never mix timeframes in your analysis—a daily bearish engulfing setup requires daily-appropriate stop placement and position management.

The Ultimate Stop-Loss

Overcoming Selling Psychological Barriers

The Comfort Challenge

Most traders never become comfortable with selling because they never practice it systematically. They cherry-pick occasional short trades during obvious bear markets, then wonder why they lack confidence when opportunity arises.

Comfort comes from repetition and success. Start by paper trading selling setups using identical methodology to your buying approach. Document your reasoning, track your theoretical results, and gradually build confidence in the process.

The News Bias Problem

Financial media has a natural bias toward bullish stories. "Market reaches new highs" generates more clicks than "Market tests support." "Economy shows growth" sells more advertising than "Warning signs emerge."

This constant bullish bombardment creates subconscious resistance to selling opportunities. You must actively counteract this bias by focusing on price action rather than narrative, structure rather than story.

The Timing Anxiety

Because bear markets move faster, traders often feel they've "missed the move" when they identify selling opportunities. This timing anxiety causes hesitation that kills potentially profitable trades.

Remember that bear markets, like bull markets, consist of waves. Missing the initial breakdown doesn't mean missing the entire move. Patient traders often find better entry points during bear market rallies than during the initial panic selling.

The Size Temptation

Fast bear market moves can tempt traders to use larger position sizes, thinking they need to "make up for lost time" or "catch the big move." This is exactly backwards.

The Ultimate Stop-Loss

Faster moves require more conservative position sizing, not more aggressive sizing. The increased volatility demands wider stops, which naturally reduces your position size for the same risk level. Accept this mathematical reality rather than fighting it.

Building Selling Confidence

Start with Paper Trading

Before risking real money on selling setups, practice with paper trades:

1. **Identify bearish engulfing patterns** on your preferred timeframes

2. **Apply stop placement methodology** exactly as you would for buying

3. **Calculate position sizes** using the same risk parameters

4. **Track results** with the same documentation standards

5. **Analyze outcomes** to build pattern recognition

Use Identical Methodology

The fastest way to build selling confidence is to use identical processes:

- Same chart analysis techniques

- Same pattern quality requirements

- Same stop placement rules (reversed)

- Same position sizing calculations

- Same trade management principles

This consistency eliminates the psychological burden of learning new systems while building new directional skills.

Focus on Process, Not Outcomes

Individual selling trades will win and lose just like buying trades. Your focus must remain on process execution rather than single-trade outcomes. A perfectly executed selling trade that hits its stop for a clean loss is more valuable than a sloppy winning trade.

The Ultimate Stop-Loss

Embrace the Speed

Instead of fearing bear market speed, embrace it as an advantage. Faster moves mean quicker feedback on your analysis, shorter time commitments, and more frequent opportunities to practice your skills.

The speed that intimidates amateur traders becomes a competitive advantage for professional traders who adapt their mindset and methodology accordingly.

The Professional Selling Mindset

Direction Agnosticism

Professional traders are direction agnostic—they profit from price movement regardless of direction. This mindset shift eliminates the emotional attachment to market direction and allows pure focus on opportunity identification and execution.

You are not a bull or a bear. You are a trader who capitalizes on market inefficiencies in both directions.

Risk Management Symmetry

Your risk management approach must be identical for buying and selling:

- Same maximum risk per trade

- Same portfolio risk limits

- Same stop loss discipline

- Same position sizing methodology

- Same emotional management techniques

The direction of the trade should never influence your risk management decisions.

The Ultimate Stop-Loss

Opportunity Recognition

Train yourself to see selling opportunities with the same clarity you see buying opportunities:

- Bearish engulfing = Bullish engulfing (reversed)

- Resistance breakdowns = Support breakouts (reversed)

- Downtrend continuations = Uptrend continuations (reversed)

- Bear flag patterns = Bull flag patterns (reversed)

Pattern recognition is pattern recognition—direction is just a variable.

Common Selling Psychology Traps

The Moral Trap

Believing that selling is somehow "wrong" or "unethical" will sabotage your ability to execute profitable selling setups. Markets need both buyers and sellers to function efficiently. You provide necessary liquidity.

The Comfort Trap

Waiting until you feel "comfortable" with selling means waiting forever. Comfort comes from experience, and experience comes from execution. Start with small positions and build confidence through successful repetition.

The Speed Trap

Trying to use buying psychology and timing in selling markets will cause you to miss entries and exit too early. Adapt your expectations to match bear market characteristics rather than forcing bear markets to match bull market psychology.

The Size Trap

Using inappropriate position sizes for increased volatility will destroy your account faster in bear markets than bull markets. Respect the mathematics of wider stops and faster moves.

The Ultimate Stop-Loss

The Direction Trap

Falling in love with one direction—whether buying or selling—limits your opportunities and clouds your judgment. Markets don't care about your directional preferences.

Preparing for Technical Application

This psychological foundation is essential before learning the technical rules for selling setups. Without the proper mindset, even perfect technical execution will fail under the pressure of real market conditions.

In the next chapter, you'll learn the Primary Rule for selling: placing stops at the last significant high. But this technical knowledge will only be effective if you've internalized the psychological principles covered here.

Mental Checklist Before Proceeding:

✓ You understand that selling is opportunity, not pessimism ✓ You accept that bear markets move faster than bull markets ✓ You're committed to using identical methodology in both directions ✓ You recognize that comfort comes from experience, not theory ✓ You embrace direction agnosticism as professional development

If any item on this checklist creates doubt or resistance, re-read this chapter before proceeding. Technical mastery without psychological mastery is a recipe for inconsistent results and emotional trading decisions.

The methodology works equally well in both directions, but only if your mind is properly prepared to execute it without bias, fear, or moral confusion.

"Bulls make money, bears make money, but pigs get slaughtered. The professional trader learns to be both bull and bear as opportunity dictates." — **Royalty FX Academy Philosophy**

The Ultimate Stop-Loss

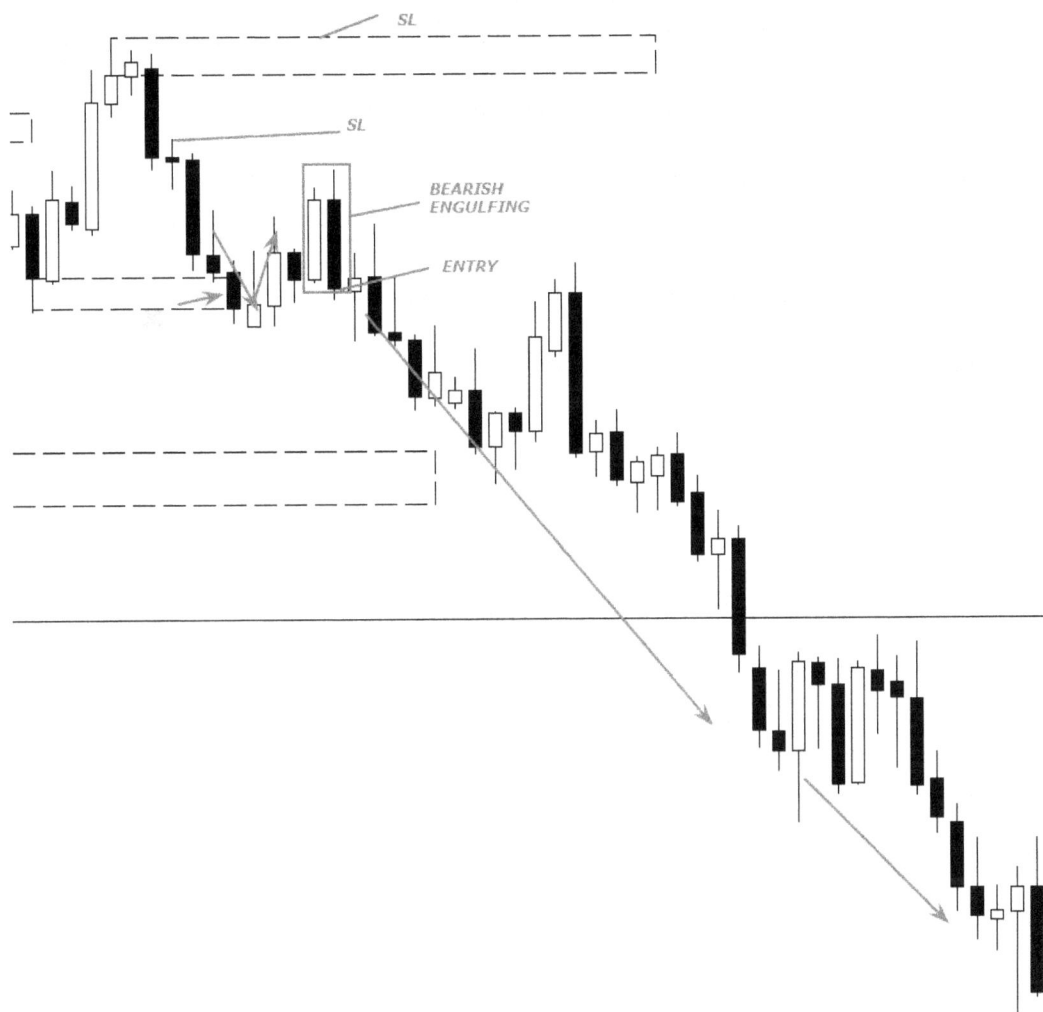

SL

SL

BEARISH
ENGULFING

ENTRY

Chapter 6: Primary Rule for Selling - Last High Placement

The Mirror Image of Success

If you mastered the Primary Rule for buying—placing stops below the last significant low—then you already understand 90% of what you need to know about selling. The Primary Rule for selling is simply the mirror image, applied with identical discipline and reasoning.

The Ultimate Stop-Loss

The Primary Rule for Selling:

When entering a selling position based on technical analysis, place your stop loss above the last significant high that defines the current market structure.

This rule forms the foundation of every selling trade you'll ever make. Every profitable short position, every protected account during bear markets, every moment of confidence while selling—all stem from understanding and applying this principle without exception.

But "mirror image" doesn't mean "automatically easy." The psychological challenges of selling require that we examine this rule with fresh eyes, understanding not just what to do, but why it works and how to apply it under pressure.

Understanding "Last Significant High"

Definition and Identification

A significant high is a price level that represents meaningful resistance or a turning point in market structure. Not every high qualifies—just as not every low qualified for buying setups.

Criteria for Significance:

Time Element: The high should be separated from current price action by meaningful time. A high from two hours ago on a daily chart setup lacks significance. A high from two weeks ago carries structural weight.

Price Reaction: The market should have shown clear reaction at or near this high. Signs include multiple touches, strong reversals, or volume expansion at the level.

Structural Role: The high should define or contribute to the current market structure. Major trend highs, range boundaries, and breakout levels typically qualify.

The Ultimate Stop-Loss

Visual Clarity: On your analysis timeframe, the high should be visually obvious. If you have to search for it or debate its significance, it probably doesn't qualify.

The Psychology Behind Last High Placement

The Crowd Psychology

Every significant high represents a price level where sellers overwhelmed buyers. Often, this occurred because buyers became exhausted, overextended, or faced unexpected resistance.

When price approaches a previous significant high, several psychological forces activate:

Trapped Buyers: Traders who bought near the previous high and held through the decline are eager to "get out even." This creates selling pressure as price approaches their break-even level.

Memory Resistance: The market remembers significant highs. Technical analysts, institutional traders, and algorithmic systems all flag these levels as potential resistance points.

Profit Taking: Traders holding profitable short positions from higher levels may take profits near previous highs, creating buying pressure that could reverse your new selling position.

Failed Break Psychology: If price breaks above the significant high, it signals that the previous resistance has become support, potentially invalidating bearish scenarios.

Why Tight Stops Fail in Selling

The Speed Problem

Bear markets move faster than bull markets, creating more volatility around entry levels. A tight stop that might work in a slowly developing bull market will get whipsawed in a fast-moving bear market.

The Ultimate Stop-Loss

The Retracement Reality

Even strong selling moves experience retracements. A 100-pip initial decline might see a 30-40 pip bounce before continuing lower. Tight stops placed 20 pips above entry will be hit during normal market breathing.

The Institutional Activity

Large players often test resistance levels before major selling campaigns. Their activity can push price temporarily above your entry point, triggering tight stops before the main move develops.

The False Break Phenomenon

Markets frequently make brief forays above resistance before failing. These false breaks are designed to trigger stop losses from weak hands before the real move begins.

Applying the Primary Rule: Step-by-Step Process

Step 1: Confirm Your Analysis Timeframe

Your stop placement must match your analysis timeframe. If you identified the selling setup on daily charts, use daily chart structure for stop placement. Don't mix timeframes.

Step 2: Identify the Last Significant High

Scan back through your analysis timeframe looking for the most recent high that meets significance criteria:

- Clear structural importance

- Meaningful time separation from current price

- Evidence of previous market reaction

- Visual obviousness on your chart

Step 3: Add Appropriate Buffer

Place your stop 10-20 pips above the identified high, depending on:

The Ultimate Stop-Loss

- Currency pair characteristics (GBP pairs need wider buffers)

- Current market volatility

- Time of day/session considerations

- Overall market environment

Step 4: Calculate Position Size

Use your predetermined risk percentage and the actual stop distance to calculate appropriate position size. Never adjust your risk to accommodate a particular position size preference.

Step 5: Document Your Reasoning

Write down which high you chose and why. This documentation will help you learn from both successful and unsuccessful trades.

Real-World Application Examples

Example 1: EUR/USD Daily Setup

Market Context: EUR/USD has been rallying from 1.0500 to 1.0850, showing signs of exhaustion at higher levels.

Current Price: 1.0825

Setup: Bearish engulfing pattern forming on daily chart

High Analysis:

- Recent high at 1.0867 (yesterday's high)

- More significant high at 1.0895 (from one week ago)

- Major structural high at 1.0950 (from three weeks ago)

Selection Process: The 1.0895 level shows the best combination of recency and significance. It held for two days, created a clear reversal, and represents the current resistance structure.

Stop Placement: 1.0905 (10 pips above 1.0895 high)

The Ultimate Stop-Loss

Reasoning: The 1.0950 level is too distant for a daily setup, while yesterday's 1.0867 high lacks structural significance.

Example 2: GBP/JPY Range Breakdown

Market Context: GBP/JPY has been ranging between 178.00 and 185.00 for six weeks.

Current Price: 177.80 (breaking below range support)

Setup: Range breakdown with bearish momentum

High Analysis:

- Range top at 185.00 (multiple touches over six weeks)

- Recent high within range at 182.50 (three days ago)

- Intraday highs at various levels

Selection Process: The 185.00 range top is the only significant high that matters for this setup. It defines the entire structure of the current market.

Stop Placement: 185.25 (25 pips above 185.00, wider buffer for GBP/JPY volatility)

Reasoning: A break above 185.00 would invalidate the range breakdown thesis entirely.

Common Mistakes in High Identification

Mistake 1: Using Intraday Levels for Swing Trades

Using a 4-hour high as a stop reference for a daily chart setup creates mismatch between analysis and execution timeframes.

Correct Approach: Match your stop timeframe to your analysis timeframe consistently.

Mistake 2: Choosing Convenient Rather Than Significant Highs

Selecting a nearby high because it creates a comfortable stop distance rather than identifying the truly significant structural level.

The Ultimate Stop-Loss

Correct Approach: Let market structure dictate stop placement, then adjust position size accordingly.

Mistake 3: Overthinking Multiple Options

Getting paralyzed when multiple potential highs exist, leading to analysis paralysis or arbitrary selection.

Correct Approach: Use the most recent high that meets all significance criteria. When in doubt, go wider rather than tighter.

Mistake 4: Ignoring Currency Pair Characteristics

Using identical buffer distances for EUR/USD and GBP/JPY despite their vastly different volatility profiles.

Correct Approach: Adjust buffers based on instrument characteristics while maintaining consistent methodology.

The Mathematics of Selling Stops

Position Sizing with Wider Stops

Selling setups often require wider stops than buying setups due to increased volatility and faster market movement. This naturally reduces your position size for the same risk level.

Example Calculation:

- Account size: $100,000

- Risk per trade: 2% = $2,000

- Entry price: 1.0825

- Stop price: 1.0905

- Stop distance: 80 pips

- Position size: 2.5 lots (to risk $2,000 over 80 pips)

Accepting Mathematical Reality

Don't fight the mathematics by:

The Ultimate Stop-Loss

- Increasing risk percentage to maintain position size

- Using tighter stops to allow larger positions

- Skipping trades because stops seem "too wide"

The mathematics are protecting you from inappropriate risk-taking.

Risk-Reward Considerations

Wider stops require larger profit targets to maintain attractive risk-reward ratios:

- 80-pip stop should target minimum 160-pip profit

- Consider multiple profit targets for position management

- Factor in faster bear market movement for achievable targets

Advanced Stop Placement Concepts

Multiple Timeframe Confirmation

While your primary analysis determines stop placement, checking higher timeframes can confirm your selection:

Daily setup with weekly confirmation: If your daily chart identifies a significant high at 1.0895, check that this level also appears significant on weekly charts.

Avoiding timeframe conflicts: Ensure your selected high doesn't conflict with obvious higher timeframe structure.

Session Considerations

Different trading sessions create different volatility patterns:

Asian Session: Lower volatility may allow tighter buffers **London Session:** Higher volatility requires wider buffers **Overlap Periods:** Increased activity demands extra caution

Economic Event Adjustments

Major news releases can create temporary volatility spikes:

The Ultimate Stop-Loss

Pre-news positioning: Consider wider buffers when holding through scheduled events **Post-news validation:** Ensure your structural high remains valid after major news

Psychology of Watching Your Stop

The Approach Anxiety

As price moves toward your stop level, anxiety naturally increases. This is normal but must be managed:

Trust your analysis: The high was chosen for structural reasons that remain valid **Avoid micro-management:** Don't watch every tick as it approaches your stop **Prepare mentally:** Accept that being stopped out is part of the methodology

The False Break Scenario

Sometimes price will break above your identified high briefly before reversing:

Stay disciplined: Don't second-guess your stop placement during the event **Wait for true break:** A few pips above doesn't invalidate your analysis **Learn from outcome:** Document what happened for future improvement

When Stops Are Hit: Analysis and Learning

Immediate Response

When your stop is triggered:

1. **Accept the loss immediately:** Don't argue with the market's decision

2. **Review your analysis:** Was the high selection appropriate?

3. **Check execution:** Was stop placement consistent with methodology?

4. **Document lessons:** What can you learn for future trades?

Post-Stop Price Action

Watch how price behaves after hitting your stop:

The Ultimate Stop-Loss

Continued rally: Your structural analysis may have been incorrect **Quick reversal:** You may have been right but with poor timing **Consolidation:** The level may still be significant despite the break

Learning Integration

Use stopped-out trades as learning opportunities:

- Was the high selection process correct?
- Should the buffer have been wider?
- Did news events influence the outcome?
- How can you improve next time?

Building Stop Placement Confidence

Start with Paper Trading

Practice identifying significant highs without financial pressure:

- Mark potential stops on historical charts
- See how they would have performed
- Build pattern recognition skills
- Develop confidence in the process

Use Consistent Methodology

Apply the same high-identification process every time:

- Same timeframe analysis
- Same significance criteria
- Same buffer calculations
- Same documentation standards

Track Your Results

Maintain records of your stop placement decisions:

The Ultimate Stop-Loss

- Which highs you selected and why

- How often stops were triggered

- Whether alternative highs would have worked better

- Overall profitability including stopped trades

Integration with Overall Strategy

Risk Management Harmony

Your stop placement must integrate seamlessly with overall risk management:

- Consistent risk percentage per trade

- Portfolio-level risk limits

- Correlation considerations across positions

- Position sizing discipline

Trade Management Planning

Know your profit targets before entering:

- Primary target based on risk-reward ratio

- Secondary targets for position scaling

- Trail stop strategy for extended moves

- Exit criteria for changing conditions

Psychological Preparation

Accept the realities of selling with structural stops:

- Some trades will be stopped out quickly

- Bear markets move fast and require patience

- Wider stops reduce position sizes

- Process consistency matters more than individual outcomes

The Ultimate Stop-Loss

Preparing for Secondary Rule

The Primary Rule handles the majority of selling situations, but markets sometimes present scenarios where alternative stop placement becomes appropriate. In the next chapter, you'll learn the Secondary Rule: when to use bearish engulfing highs instead of structural highs.

Understanding when to deviate from the Primary Rule requires complete mastery of the Primary Rule itself. The decision matrix you'll learn in Chapter 7 assumes you can identify significant highs quickly and confidently.

Mastery Checklist:

Before proceeding to Chapter 7, ensure you can:

✓ Identify significant highs on any timeframe ✓ Distinguish between structural and temporary highs ✓ Calculate appropriate buffers for different currency pairs ✓ Size positions correctly based on actual stop distances ✓ Accept that wider stops reduce position sizes ✓ Document your reasoning for each stop placement decision

The Primary Rule for selling will handle 80% of your short setups. Master it completely before learning when exceptions apply.

"The market's memory lives in significant highs and lows. Trade with that memory, not against it, and the market will reward your respect for its structure." **— Royalty FX Academy Philosophy**

The Ultimate Stop-Loss

SL

BEARISH
ENGULFING

ENTRY

Chapter 7: Secondary Rule for Selling - Bearish Engulfing High Placement

Beyond the Primary Rule

The Primary Rule for selling—placing stops above the last significant high—handles the vast majority of short setups with mathematical precision and psychological soundness. But markets occasionally present scenarios where rigid adherence to structural highs creates inefficiency, excessive risk, or missed opportunities.

Just as buying setups sometimes require secondary consideration, selling setups demand flexible thinking within a disciplined framework.

The Secondary Rule for Selling:

When the distance to the last significant high creates excessive risk relative to the setup's potential, or when market structure suggests the bearish engulfing high itself represents the most relevant resistance level, place your stop above the high of the bearish engulfing pattern that created your entry signal.

This rule doesn't replace the Primary Rule—it supplements it. Understanding when to apply which rule separates consistently profitable traders from those who rigidly apply single solutions to dynamic market conditions.

When the Primary Rule Creates Problems

Problem 1: Excessive Risk Distance

Sometimes the last significant high sits so far above your entry that even minimum position sizing creates uncomfortable risk exposure.

Example Scenario:

- EUR/USD bearish engulfing at 1.0825

- Last significant high at 1.1150 (325 pips away)

- 2% account risk = $2,000

The Ultimate Stop-Loss

- Minimum position size = 0.6 lots

- Even small position creates outsized trade impact

Problem 2: Structural Irrelevance

Occasionally, the last significant high reflects outdated market conditions that no longer influence current price action.

Example Scenario:

- GBP/JPY forming bearish engulfing at 178.50

- Last significant high at 185.00 from two months ago

- Multiple structural changes since that high

- Recent range trading between 177.00-180.00

- 185.00 level no longer relevant to current dynamics

Problem 3: Timeframe Mismatch

When your analysis timeframe creates stops that don't match the setup's characteristics or expected duration.

Example Scenario:

- Daily chart bearish engulfing setup

- Expected 2-3 day trade duration

- Last significant high from weekly structure

- Stop distance appropriate for monthly holding period

- Mismatch between setup timeframe and stop timeframe

Understanding Bearish Engulfing High Placement

The Logic

The bearish engulfing pattern represents a complete reversal of the previous bar's bullish sentiment. The high of this engulfing bar marks the precise point where bears overwhelmed bulls and seized control.

The Ultimate Stop-Loss

If your analysis suggests that this reversal point carries more structural significance than distant historical levels, the engulfing high becomes your logical stop reference.

Psychological Foundation

The engulfing high represents fresh resistance created by the current market dynamics. Buyers who got trapped at that high level have immediate reason to sell if price returns there. The memory is fresh, the pain is recent, and the technical significance is clear.

Time Sensitivity

Unlike historical significant highs that maintain relevance for weeks or months, engulfing highs carry time-sensitive significance. Their importance diminishes as market dynamics evolve, making them most effective for shorter-duration trades.

The Decision Matrix: Primary vs. Secondary

Use Primary Rule (Last Significant High) When:

✓ **Distance is reasonable:** Stop distance allows appropriate position sizing ✓ **High remains relevant:** The structural level still influences current price action ✓ **Timeframe matches:** Your analysis timeframe aligns with the structural high's timeframe ✓ **Clean structure:** The significant high is clearly defined and unambiguous ✓ **Standard volatility:** Market conditions don't suggest unusual volatility patterns

Use Secondary Rule (Engulfing High) When:

✓ **Distance is excessive:** Primary rule creates position sizes below practical minimums ✓ **Structure has changed:** Multiple developments since the last significant high ✓ **Timeframe mismatch:** Expected trade duration doesn't match structural timeframe ✓ **Engulfing significance:** The pattern high carries clear technical importance ✓ **Recent resistance:** The engulfing high represents the most current resistance level

The Ultimate Stop-Loss

Never Use Secondary Rule When:

✗ You're trying to avoid a legitimate stop distance for emotional reasons ✗ The engulfing high lacks any technical significance ✗ You're cherry-picking rules to increase position size ✗ The Primary Rule creates reasonable risk parameters ✗ You haven't thoroughly analyzed the structural high

Application Process: Step-by-Step

Step 1: Apply Primary Rule Analysis

Always start with the Primary Rule:

1. Identify the last significant high

2. Calculate the stop distance

3. Determine required position size

4. Assess reasonableness of risk parameters

Step 2: Evaluate Secondary Rule Criteria

Only if Primary Rule creates problems:

1. Is the distance genuinely excessive for the setup?

2. Has market structure changed significantly since the last high?

3. Does the engulfing high carry technical significance?

4. Would Secondary Rule create more appropriate risk parameters?

Step 3: Make the Decision

Choose based on which rule better serves the setup:

- **Primary Rule:** When structural analysis supports it and risk is reasonable

- **Secondary Rule:** Only when Primary Rule creates genuine inefficiency

The Ultimate Stop-Loss

Step 4: Execute with Commitment

Once you choose a rule, execute it completely:

- Don't second-guess during the trade

- Don't switch rules mid-trade

- Document your reasoning for future review

Real-World Application Examples

Example 1: EUR/USD - Secondary Rule Application

Market Context: EUR/USD has been declining from 1.1500 over six weeks, currently consolidating between 1.0800-1.0900.

Setup: Daily bearish engulfing pattern at 1.0875

- Previous bar: Small bullish bar closing at 1.0870

- Engulfing bar: Opens at 1.0873, reaches high of 1.0887, closes at 1.0855

- Pattern quality: Clean engulfment with strong close

Primary Rule Analysis:

- Last significant high: 1.1150 (from three weeks ago)

- Stop distance: 275 pips to 1.1165

- Position size for 2% risk: 0.73 lots

- Assessment: Distance excessive for consolidation breakdown

Secondary Rule Analysis:

- Engulfing high: 1.0887

- Technical significance: Clear resistance within current range structure

- Stop distance: 15 pips to 1.0902

- Position size for 2% risk: 13.3 lots

The Ultimate Stop-Loss

- Assessment: More appropriate for expected move

Decision: Secondary Rule **Reasoning:** The 1.1150 level reflects the broader trend but isn't relevant for current range dynamics. The engulfing high at 1.0887 represents immediate resistance within the consolidation pattern.

Trade Execution:

- Entry: 1.0875 (current price)

- Stop: 1.0902 (15 pips above engulfing high)

- Position: 13.3 lots (2% risk over 15 pips)

- Target: 1.0800 (range support, 75 pips profit potential)

Example 2: GBP/USD - Primary Rule Maintained

Market Context: GBP/USD showing bearish engulfing on daily chart after failing at major resistance.

Setup: Daily bearish engulfing at 1.2650

- Previous bar: Bullish bar closing at 1.2655

- Engulfing bar: Opens at 1.2660, reaches 1.2675, closes at 1.2635

- Pattern quality: Strong engulfment with conviction close

Primary Rule Analysis:

- Last significant high: 1.2750 (from one week ago)

- Stop distance: 105 pips to 1.2765

- Position size for 2% risk: 1.9 lots

- Assessment: Reasonable distance for swing trade setup

Secondary Rule Analysis:

- Engulfing high: 1.2675

- Stop distance: 30 pips to 1.2690

The Ultimate Stop-Loss

- Position size for 2% risk: 6.7 lots

- Assessment: Would allow larger position but...

Decision: Primary Rule **Reasoning:** The 1.2750 level represents genuine structural resistance that influenced the current setup. The shorter stop to the engulfing high doesn't provide adequate protection against structural breaks.

Trade Execution:

- Entry: 1.2650 (current price)

- Stop: 1.2765 (15 pips above structural high)

- Position: 1.9 lots (2% risk over 105 pips)

- Target: 1.2440 (major support, 210 pips profit potential)

Advanced Decision-Making Scenarios

Scenario 1: Multiple Timeframe Conflict

Situation: Daily bearish engulfing conflicts with weekly structure

- Daily setup suggests Secondary Rule application

- Weekly structure supports Primary Rule approach

- Trader must choose primary analysis timeframe

Resolution Process:

1. Identify your primary decision timeframe

2. Stick with that timeframe's rule selection

3. Don't mix timeframes in single trade decisions

4. Accept the mathematical consequences

Scenario 2: Economic Event Proximity

Situation: Major news release scheduled during trade timeframe

The Ultimate Stop-Loss

- Normal analysis suggests Secondary Rule

- News volatility might spike price through close stops

- Event timing influences rule selection

Resolution Process:

1. Assess news impact probability

2. Consider wider buffers regardless of rule choice

3. Potentially defer trade until after event

4. Don't let news fear override good analysis

Scenario 3: Market Session Transitions

Situation: Setup occurs during session transition

- Asian session: Lower volatility supports Secondary Rule

- London open: Higher volatility suggests Primary Rule

- Timing influences risk assessment

Resolution Process:

1. Match stop placement to expected volatility

2. Consider session characteristics in buffer calculation

3. Adjust position size for session-specific risks

4. Maintain rule consistency within chosen framework

Common Secondary Rule Mistakes

Mistake 1: Convenience Selection

Using Secondary Rule because Primary Rule seems "too wide" without legitimate structural analysis.

Correct Approach: Apply decision matrix objectively, not emotionally.

Mistake 2: Position Size Manipulation

The Ultimate Stop-Loss

Choosing Secondary Rule to allow larger position sizes rather than accepting appropriate risk.

Correct Approach: Let risk management dictate position size, not position preference dictate risk.

Mistake 3: Inconsistent Application

Switching between rules arbitrarily or changing rules mid-trade based on price action.

Correct Approach: Make rule decisions before entering and commit to them completely.

Mistake 4: Ignoring Buffer Requirements

Placing stops exactly at engulfing highs without appropriate buffers for volatility.

Correct Approach: Always add appropriate buffers regardless of which rule you use.

Risk Management with Secondary Rule

Position Sizing Implications

Secondary Rule typically creates shorter stop distances, which mathematically allows larger position sizes. This can be both opportunity and trap.

Opportunity Benefits:

- More efficient risk utilization

- Better risk-reward ratios for shorter-term moves

- Increased position flexibility

Trap Dangers:

- Overleverage temptation

- Inadequate protection against structural breaks

The Ultimate Stop-Loss

- False sense of security from tight stops

Balanced Approach:

Use the mathematical advantage wisely:

- Take smaller profits more frequently

- Scale positions more actively

- Maintain overall portfolio risk limits

- Don't increase individual trade risk percentages

Buffer Calculations

Engulfing highs require buffers just like structural highs:

Standard Buffers:

- EUR/USD: 8-12 pips

- GBP/USD: 15-20 pips

- GBP/JPY: 20-30 pips

- USD/JPY: 10-15 pips

Volatility Adjustments:

- High volatility periods: Add 50% to standard buffer

- Major news proximity: Consider doubling buffer

- Session overlap periods: Add 25% to buffer

- Weekend gap risk: Factor in gap potential

Trade Management Considerations

Profit Targets with Secondary Rule

Shorter stops often require adjusted profit expectations:

Target Calculation:

The Ultimate Stop-Loss

- Minimum 2:1 risk-reward ratio

- Consider multiple profit levels

- Account for faster bear market movement

- Plan position scaling strategy

Stop Management Evolution

Secondary Rule stops may need faster adjustment:

Trail Strategy:

- Move to breakeven more quickly

- Use smaller trail increments

- Consider time-based adjustments

- Monitor structural level development

Exit Criteria Adaptation

Short-term oriented stops require short-term oriented exits:

Time Management:

- Don't expect extended holding periods

- Take profits more aggressively

- Monitor for pattern completion

- Exit on momentum loss

Building Secondary Rule Competence

Practice Sequence:

1. **Master Primary Rule completely** before considering Secondary Rule

2. **Study historical examples** of both rule applications

3. **Paper trade decision matrix** until selections become intuitive

4. **Start with small positions** when applying Secondary Rule with real money

5. **Document all decisions** for continuous improvement

Decision Checklist:

Before choosing Secondary Rule, confirm: ✓ Primary Rule creates genuine inefficiency ✓ Engulfing high has technical significance ✓ Market structure supports shorter-term approach ✓ Risk management remains appropriate ✓ You're not rationalizing convenience

Competence Indicators:

You're ready to use Secondary Rule when:

- Primary Rule decisions are automatic

- You can identify structural significance quickly

- Position sizing calculations are intuitive

- Risk management discipline is unbreakable

- You understand both rules' psychological foundations

Integration with Overall Methodology

Consistency Principles:

Whether using Primary or Secondary Rule:

- Risk percentage per trade remains identical

- Position sizing mathematics stay consistent

- Trade documentation standards don't change

- Psychological discipline requirements are equal

- Overall portfolio limits still apply

Rule Selection Documentation:

For every trade, record:

- Which rule you chose and why

- Alternative rule's parameters for comparison

- Market conditions influencing decision

- Outcome analysis for both rules

- Lessons learned for future application

Preparing for Case Studies

Understanding when to use Secondary Rule requires seeing both rules applied in real market conditions. In Chapter 8, you'll see complete trade examples showing:

- Primary Rule successes and failures

- Secondary Rule applications and outcomes

- Decision-making processes in real time

- Risk management across both approaches

- Psychological challenges and solutions

The Secondary Rule is a tool, not a crutch. It exists to optimize your trading within sound risk management principles, not to circumvent them. Use it judiciously, document your decisions, and always prioritize protection over profit.

"Flexibility within discipline creates opportunity. Discipline without flexibility creates rigidity. Master both rules, but never compromise the principles that govern them." **— Royalty FX Academy Philosophy**

The Ultimate Stop-Loss

SL

BEARISH ENGULFING
*it took 4 canales to engulf
the last bullish cndle*

ENTRY

LAST LOW

ROYALTY FX
ACADEMY

Chapter 8: Real-Life Selling Case Studies

Learning Through Market Reality

Theory becomes wisdom only through application. Charts become profitable only through execution. Rules become instinct only through repetition under real market pressure.

This chapter presents complete selling trade case studies drawn from actual market conditions, showing you exactly how professional traders identify setups, apply stop placement rules, manage positions, and handle the psychological challenges that separate successful traders from the struggling majority.

Each case study includes complete analysis, real-time decision making, position management, and post-trade review. You'll see both successful trades and educational losses, both Primary and Secondary Rule applications, and both smooth executions and challenging management scenarios.

Study these examples not as entertainment, but as blueprints for your own trading development.

Case Study 1: EUR/USD Daily Bearish Engulfing - Primary Rule Success

Market Context (Day 1 - Analysis)

EUR/USD has been consolidating between 1.0850 and 1.0950 for three weeks following a decline from 1.1200. The pair is approaching the upper boundary of this range with diminishing momentum.

Setup Identification:

- **Timeframe:** Daily chart analysis

- **Previous bar:** Small bullish doji closing at 1.0943, showing indecision near range top

- **Current bar (in progress):** Opening at 1.0945, reaching high of 1.0952, currently trading at 1.0915

The Ultimate Stop-Loss

- **Pattern recognition:** Potential bearish engulfing if close occurs below 1.0935

Primary Rule Analysis:

- **Last significant high:** 1.0965 (from two weeks ago, multiple touches, clear resistance)

- **Technical significance:** Defined the range top, showed multiple rejections

- **Time relevance:** Recent enough to remain structurally significant

- **Stop placement:** 1.0975 (10 pips above 1.0965 high)

Secondary Rule Consideration:

- **Engulfing high:** 1.0952 (if pattern completes)

- **Distance comparison:** Primary = 60 pips, Secondary = 37 pips

- **Decision:** Primary Rule appropriate - distance reasonable, structure clear

Trade Plan Development:

- **Entry trigger:** Close below 1.0935 confirming bearish engulfing

- **Stop loss:** 1.0975 (Primary Rule application)

- **Position size:** 3.33 lots (2% risk over 60 pips = $2,000 ÷ $6/pip = 333 mini lots)

- **Primary target:** 1.0850 (range support, 85 pips profit = $2,833)

- **Risk-reward ratio:** 1.42:1 (acceptable for range breakdown)

Market Close Analysis: Final bar: Opens 1.0945, High 1.0952, Low 1.0912, Close 1.0918 Pattern confirmation: ✓ Complete bearish engulfment (close 1.0918 < previous close 1.0943)

Day 2 - Trade Execution

The Ultimate Stop-Loss

Entry: 1.0918 (market open, confirming yesterday's close) **Stop:** 1.0975 **Size:** 3.33 lots **Mental state:** Confident in setup quality and risk management

Day 2-4 - Position Management

Day 2: Price declines to 1.0895, holds above 1.0890 support **Day 3:** Further decline to 1.0872, approaching target zone **Day 4:** Price reaches 1.0857, near primary target

Management Decision: Take 50% profit at 1.0857 (61 pips = $2,033 profit), trail remaining position with stop at 1.0935 (breakeven + 17 pips profit protection)

Day 5-7 - Position Resolution

Day 5: Price bounces to 1.0881, holds below resistance **Day 6:** Renewed selling pressure, price falls to 1.0834 **Day 7:** Strong decline continues to 1.0815

Final Exit: Close remaining 50% position at 1.0815 (103 pips = $1,717 additional profit)

Trade Results:

- **Total profit:** $3,750 ($2,033 + $1,717)

- **Risk taken:** $2,000

- **Actual return:** 1.875:1 risk-reward

- **Trade duration:** 7 days

- **Execution quality:** Excellent

Key Success Factors:

1. **Patient setup identification:** Waited for complete pattern confirmation

2. **Appropriate rule selection:** Primary Rule provided adequate protection

The Ultimate Stop-Loss

3. **Disciplined position sizing:** Risk management maintained throughout

4. **Strategic profit taking:** Secured profits while allowing extended move

5. **Emotional control:** No second-guessing or premature exits

Learning Points:

- Range breakdowns can provide extended moves beyond initial targets

- Primary Rule protection allowed comfortable position holding

- Partial profit taking reduced emotional pressure on remaining position

- Documentation helped maintain objectivity throughout trade

Case Study 2: GBP/JPY Bearish Engulfing - Secondary Rule Application

Market Context (Day 1 - Analysis)

GBP/JPY has been volatile, ranging between 178.00 and 182.00 for ten days. A bearish engulfing pattern is forming at 179.50, but the last significant high sits much higher at 185.20 from a previous trend.

Setup Identification:

- **Timeframe:** Daily chart

- **Previous bar:** Bullish bar closing at 179.65

- **Current bar:** Opens 179.70, high 180.15, currently trading 179.20

- **Pattern quality:** Strong bearish engulfment developing

Primary Rule Analysis:

- **Last significant high:** 185.20 (from five weeks ago)

- **Stop distance:** 580 pips to 185.30

- **Position size:** 0.34 lots (2% risk ÷ $58/pip = 34 mini lots)

- **Assessment:** Extremely small position size for range-bound setup

The Ultimate Stop-Loss

Secondary Rule Analysis:

- **Engulfing high:** 180.15 (current bar high)

- **Technical significance:** Recent resistance within current range structure

- **Stop distance:** 70 pips to 180.25

- **Position size:** 2.86 lots (2% risk ÷ $7/pip = 286 mini lots)

- **Assessment:** More appropriate sizing for expected range move

Decision Matrix Application: ✓ Distance excessive with Primary Rule ✓ Market structure changed significantly since 185.20 high ✓ Engulfing high represents current resistance level ✓ Expected trade duration matches Secondary Rule timeframe

Decision: Secondary Rule application justified

Trade Plan:

- **Entry:** 179.50 (on close confirmation)

- **Stop:** 180.25 (10 pips above engulfing high)

- **Position:** 2.86 lots

- **Target:** 178.00 (range support, 150 pips = $4,290)

- **Risk-reward:** 2.14:1

Market Close: Bar closes at 179.35, confirming bearish engulfing

Day 2-3 - Trade Execution and Early Management

Entry: 179.35 (market open) **Initial movement:** Price drops quickly to 179.10, then bounces to 179.55

Psychological challenge: Price approaching stop level on Day 2 created anxiety, but trader maintained discipline based on Secondary Rule logic.

Day 3: Price stabilizes around 179.20, showing respect for engulfing high resistance

The Ultimate Stop-Loss

Day 4-6 - Profitable Development

Day 4: Breakdown accelerates, price falls to 178.80 **Day 5:** Continued selling to 178.45 **Day 6:** Target zone reached at 178.15

Management decision: Take 70% profit at 178.15 (120 pips = $2,400), trail remaining 30% with stop at 179.00

Day 7-8 - Position Completion

Day 7: Price bounces to 178.90, testing trail stop **Day 8:** Renewed selling pressure takes price to 177.65

Final exit: Close remaining position at 177.65 (170 pips additional = $1,428)

Trade Results:

- **Total profit:** $3,828 ($2,400 + $1,428)

- **Risk taken:** $2,000

- **Return:** 1.914:1 risk-reward

- **Duration:** 8 days

Secondary Rule Validation:

- Stop at 180.25 was never tested

- Primary Rule stop at 185.30 was never approached

- Position size optimization allowed better profit capture

- Range-focused analysis proved correct

Key Success Factors:

1. **Proper rule selection:** Secondary Rule matched setup characteristics

2. **Structural analysis:** Recognized that distant high was irrelevant

3. **Position sizing optimization:** Larger size captured range move effectively

4. **Management discipline:** Stuck with plan despite early volatility

Case Study 3: USD/JPY Failed Setup - Primary Rule Protection

Market Context (Day 1 - Analysis)

USD/JPY showing potential bearish engulfing at 149.80 after reaching 150.20 high. Setup appears clean, but this case demonstrates how proper stop placement protects capital during failed analysis.

Setup Analysis:

- **Pattern:** Bearish engulfing forming at 149.80

- **Previous bar:** Bullish close at 149.85

- **Current bar:** High 149.95, trading at 149.65

Primary Rule Application:

- **Last significant high:** 150.20 (from three days ago)

- **Stop placement:** 150.35 (15 pips above high)

- **Position size:** 3.64 lots (2% risk over 55 pips)

Trade Execution (Day 2):

- **Entry:** 149.80

- **Stop:** 150.35

- **Target:** 148.50 (130 pips profit potential)

Day 2-3 - Initial Favorable Movement

Day 2: Price declines to 149.45, setup appears to be working **Day 3:** Further decline to 149.20, trader feeling confident

Day 4 - Reversal Begins

Day 4: Unexpected economic data triggers JPY weakness

- Price gaps up to 149.95 at open

The Ultimate Stop-Loss

- Continues rising to 150.10

- Closes at 150.05

Psychological pressure: Stop level approaching, trader considers moving stop higher

Discipline maintained: Trader remembers that stop placement was based on structural analysis, not current price action

Day 5 - Stop Triggered

Day 5: Price opens at 150.15, immediately triggering stop at 150.35 **Exit:** 150.35 (55 pip loss = $2,000)

Day 5-10 - Post-Stop Analysis

Price continues rising:

- Day 6: 150.85

- Day 8: 151.50

- Day 10: 152.20

Validation of stop placement: The break above 150.20 indicated that the bearish analysis was incorrect. The Primary Rule stop protected against much larger losses.

Trade Results:

- **Loss:** $2,000 (exactly as planned)

- **Alternative scenario:** Without stop, loss would have been $2,400+ and growing

- **Risk management success:** Capital preserved for future opportunities

Key Learning Points:

1. **Stop discipline saves accounts:** Temptation to move stops would have increased losses

2. **Structural breaks matter:** Price above 150.20 invalidated bearish thesis

3. **Failed setups provide education:** Understanding why analysis failed improves future decisions

4. **Capital preservation priority:** Living to trade another day matters more than being right

---

Case Study 4: EUR/GBP Secondary Rule Failure - Learning Experience

Market Context

EUR/GBP bearish engulfing at 0.8650, but this case shows when Secondary Rule application leads to premature stop-outs and missed opportunities.

Setup Analysis:

- **Pattern:** Clean bearish engulfing at 0.8650

- **Primary Rule:** Last significant high at 0.8720 (70 pip stop)

- **Secondary Rule:** Engulfing high at 0.8665 (18 pip stop)

Rule Selection Error: Trader chose Secondary Rule to "get better risk-reward" rather than for legitimate structural reasons.

Trade Execution:

- **Entry:** 0.8650

- **Stop:** 0.8668 (Secondary Rule + buffer)

- **Size:** 11.11 lots (oversized due to tight stop)

Day 1-2 - Quick Stop Out

Day 1: Price spikes to 0.8670, triggering stop **Loss:** $2,000

Day 3-7 - Missed Opportunity

Price proceeds to fall exactly as originally analyzed:

- Day 3: 0.8620

- Day 5: 0.8590

- Day 7: 0.8560

Had Primary Rule been used:

- Stop would not have been hit

- Profit would have been $3,600+

- Risk-reward would have been 1.8:1

Critical Learning Points:

1. **Rule selection must be structural, not convenient**

2. **Secondary Rule requires legitimate justification**

3. **Tight stops don't automatically create better trades**

4. **Position sizing discipline prevents this type of error**

Case Study 5: GBP/USD Multiple Timeframe Confirmation

Market Context

This advanced case study shows how multiple timeframe analysis enhances stop placement decisions for selling setups.

Daily Chart Analysis:

- **Setup:** Bearish engulfing at 1.2750

- **Last significant high:** 1.2850 (100 pip stop distance)

Weekly Chart Confirmation:

- **Resistance confluence:** 1.2850 daily high aligns with weekly resistance zone

- **Structural significance:** Level represents major trend line intersection

The Ultimate Stop-Loss

- **Primary Rule validation:** Weekly structure confirms daily analysis

Trade Execution:

- **Entry:** 1.2750

- **Stop:** 1.2865 (Primary Rule with weekly confirmation)

- **Size:** 2.0 lots

- **Confidence level:** High due to multiple timeframe agreement

Result:

- **Successful trade:** Price fell to 1.2580 (170 pips profit)

- **Stop never tested:** Weekly resistance held significance

- **Risk-reward achieved:** 1.7:1 actual return

Multiple Timeframe Benefits:

1. **Increased confidence:** Alignment reduces second-guessing

2. **Better stop placement:** Higher timeframe structure more reliable

3. **Improved risk-reward:** Stronger resistance allows wider targets

4. **Psychological comfort:** Multiple confirmations reduce anxiety

---

Case Study 6: News Event Impact on Stop Placement

Market Context

EUR/USD bearish engulfing setup coincides with ECB announcement, demonstrating how news events influence stop placement decisions.

Setup Analysis:

- **Pattern:** Bearish engulfing at 1.0925

- **Primary Rule stop:** 1.0985 (60 pip distance)

- **News event:** ECB rate decision in 24 hours

The Ultimate Stop-Loss

Risk Assessment:

- **Normal buffer:** 10 pips above high

- **News volatility buffer:** Additional 15 pips

- **Final stop:** 1.1000 (75 pip total distance)

Position Size Adjustment:

- **Normal size:** 3.33 lots for 60 pip stop

- **News-adjusted size:** 2.67 lots for 75 pip stop

- **Risk maintained:** Still 2% of account

Trade Outcome:

- **ECB announcement:** More hawkish than expected

- **Price spike:** Reached 1.0995 (within normal buffer range)

- **News buffer protection:** Wide stop prevented whipsaw

- **Subsequent move:** Price fell to 1.0780 as analyzed

News Event Lessons:

1. **Buffer adjustments necessary:** News creates temporary volatility spikes

2. **Position size must adjust:** Wider stops require smaller positions

3. **Patience pays:** Extra protection allows riding through news noise

4. **Analysis remains valid:** Fundamental spikes don't invalidate technical setups

The Ultimate Stop-Loss

Common Patterns Across All Case Studies

Success Factors:

1. **Disciplined rule application:** Following methodology regardless of emotional pressure

2. **Appropriate position sizing:** Never compromising risk management for position preference

3. **Structural analysis quality:** Basing decisions on legitimate technical levels

4. **Management consistency:** Maintaining planned approach throughout trades

5. **Learning orientation:** Treating both wins and losses as educational experiences

Failure Factors:

1. **Convenience-based decisions:** Choosing rules to fit desired position sizes

2. **Emotional interference:** Allowing fear or greed to override methodology

3. **Inadequate preparation:** Failing to analyze all relevant structural levels

4. **Inconsistent execution:** Changing plans mid-trade without valid reasons

5. **Risk management violations:** Adjusting risk parameters for individual trades

The Ultimate Stop-Loss

Psychological Insights from Real Trading

The Approach Phase:

Every case study showed increased anxiety as price approached stop levels. Successful traders acknowledged this anxiety but maintained discipline based on their original analysis.

The Decision Moment:

Rule selection proved crucial in every case. Traders who chose rules based on structural analysis generally succeeded, while those who chose based on convenience generally failed.

The Management Challenge:

Position management separated good trades from great trades. Partial profit taking and strategic stop adjustment allowed extended profit capture without sacrificing capital protection.

The Learning Process:

Both successful and failed trades provided valuable education. Traders who documented their reasoning and reviewed outcomes improved faster than those who simply moved to the next trade.

Building Your Case Study Library

Documentation Standards:

For every selling trade you take:

1. **Pre-trade analysis:** Which rule you chose and why

2. **Market context:** What structural levels influenced your decision

3. **Risk management:** Actual position size and stop placement reasoning

4. **Psychological state:** How you felt during setup identification and execution

5. **Management decisions:** When and why you adjusted positions

6. **Post-trade review:** What you learned regardless of outcome

Review Process:

Weekly review sessions should include:

- Rule selection accuracy

- Stop placement effectiveness

- Position sizing discipline

- Management decision quality

- Psychological challenges encountered

- Lessons learned for future application

Continuous Improvement:

Your personal case study library becomes your most valuable trading resource. Patterns will emerge showing your strengths and weaknesses, successful methodologies and problematic tendencies.

Integration with Overall Trading Plan

Portfolio Context:

Individual selling trades must fit within overall portfolio management:

- **Correlation limits:** Don't overconcentrate in similar currency exposures

- **Risk allocation:** Balance selling positions with buying positions

- **Market condition adaptation:** Adjust methodology for different volatility regimes

- **Capital preservation:** Maintain overall account protection regardless of individual opportunities

System Development:

These case studies should inform your personal trading system:

The Ultimate Stop-Loss

- Which rule works better for your trading style?

- What market conditions suit your psychology?

- How do you handle the stress of approaching stops?

- What position sizes allow you to sleep comfortably?

- Which timeframes provide the best risk-reward for your patience level?

Risk Tolerance Calibration:

Every trader's risk tolerance is different. These case studies help you understand:

- **Financial tolerance:** What dollar amounts create emotional interference?

- **Technical tolerance:** How much heat can you take before panic sets in?

- **Time tolerance:** How long can you hold positions without overanalyzing?

- **Psychological tolerance:** What market conditions challenge your discipline most?

Case Study 7: AUD/USD Weekend Gap Management

Market Context (Friday Close)

AUD/USD showing bearish engulfing at 0.6750 on Friday afternoon, with Australian employment data scheduled for release during weekend Asian session.

Setup Analysis:

- **Pattern:** Clean bearish engulfing at 0.6750

- **Primary Rule:** Last significant high at 0.6820 (70 pip stop)

- **Weekend risk:** Australian data could create gap opening

The Ultimate Stop-Loss

Risk Management Adaptation:

Normal Approach:

- Entry: 0.6750

- Stop: 0.6830 (10 pip buffer above 0.6820 high)

- Size: 2.86 lots

Weekend Gap Adjustment:

- Potential gap risk: 30 pips adverse

- Adjusted stop: 0.6860 (additional 30 pip gap buffer)

- Adjusted size: 2.0 lots (maintaining 2% total risk)

- Trade-off: Lower position size for gap protection

Monday Opening:

Gap Reality:

- Friday close: 0.6750

- Monday open: 0.6735 (15 pip favorable gap)

- Australian employment: Better than expected

- Price action: Initial spike to 0.6765, then decline

Trade Development:

- Gap provided favorable entry improvement

- Stop never threatened despite news spike

- Price proceeded to 0.6685 over three days

Results:

- **Profit:** 65 pips × 2.0 lots = $1,300

- **Risk taken:** $2,000 (account for gap potential)

The Ultimate Stop-Loss

- **Actual risk-reward:** 0.65:1 (gap buffer reduced theoretical return)

Weekend Gap Lessons:

1. **Factor gap potential:** Major news can create significant opening gaps

2. **Adjust position sizing:** Reduce size to account for gap risk

3. **Don't avoid good setups:** Proper adjustment allows participation

4. **Document gap outcomes:** Build database of gap behavior for each currency pair

---

Case Study 8: CHF/JPY High Volatility Adaptation

Market Context

CHF/JPY bearish engulfing during period of extreme volatility (VIX above 30, major central bank interventions occurring).

Standard Approach Adaptation:

Normal Conditions:

- CHF/JPY standard buffer: 25 pips

- Expected daily range: 80-120 pips

High Volatility Period:

- Intraday ranges: 200+ pips

- Whipsaw frequency: Significantly increased

- Buffer requirement: 50+ pips

Setup Analysis:

- **Pattern:** Bearish engulfing at 165.50

- **Last significant high:** 167.20

- **Normal stop:** 167.45 (25 pip buffer)

The Ultimate Stop-Loss

- **Volatility-adjusted stop:** 167.70 (50 pip buffer)

Position Size Mathematics:

- **Normal volatility:** 1.95 pips (2% ÷ 195 pip risk)

- **High volatility:** 0.91 lots (2% ÷ 220 pip risk)

- **Trade-off:** Significantly smaller position for adequate protection

Trade Execution and Management:

Day 1-2: Extreme volatility

- Price swings: 165.50 to 167.60 to 164.80

- Normal stop would have been triggered multiple times

- Volatility-adjusted stop: Never threatened

Day 3-5: Volatility subsides

- Directional movement begins

- Price declines steadily to 163.70

- Target achieved: 180 pips profit

Results:

- **Profit:** 180 pips × 0.91 lots = $1,638

- **Risk taken:** $2,000

- **Volatility protection:** Successful navigation of extreme conditions

High Volatility Lessons:

1. **Adapt buffers to conditions:** Market volatility requires buffer adjustment

2. **Accept smaller positions:** Proper protection reduces position size

3. **Patience pays premium:** Waiting through volatility leads to cleaner moves

4. **Monitor VIX and similar indicators:** External volatility measures inform forex decisions

---

Case Study 9: Correlation Risk Management - EUR/USD and GBP/USD

Market Setup

Simultaneous bearish engulfing patterns on EUR/USD and GBP/USD, demonstrating proper correlation risk management.

Individual Trade Analysis:

EUR/USD Setup:

- Bearish engulfing at 1.0850

- Primary Rule stop: 1.0920 (70 pip risk)

- Individual position size: 2.86 lots (for 2% risk)

GBP/USD Setup:

- Bearish engulfing at 1.2650

- Primary Rule stop: 1.2730 (80 pip risk)

- Individual position size: 2.5 lots (for 2% risk)

Correlation Considerations:

Historical Correlation:

- EUR/USD and GBP/USD: 85% positive correlation

- Both driven by USD strength cycles

- Risk of simultaneous adverse movement

Portfolio Risk Calculation:

- **Independent assumption:** 4% total account risk (2% + 2%)

- **Reality with 85% correlation:** Approximately 3.4% actual risk

- **Conservative approach:** Treat as single 3.4% trade

Position Adjustment:

- **EUR/USD:** Reduce to 2.0 lots (1.4% individual risk)

- **GBP/USD:** Reduce to 1.75 lots (1.4% individual risk)

- **Combined risk:** 2.8% (accounting for correlation)

Trade Outcomes:

- **EUR/USD:** 95 pip profit = $1,900

- **GBP/USD:** 110 pip profit = $1,925

- **Total profit:** $3,825

- **Total risk taken:** $2,800 (correlation-adjusted)

- **Risk-reward achieved:** 1.37:1

Correlation Management Lessons:

1. **Don't double-count risk:** Highly correlated pairs create concentrated risk

2. **Reduce individual position sizes:** Maintain total portfolio risk limits

3. **Monitor correlation coefficients:** Relationships change over time

4. **Consider timing differences:** Sometimes one pair leads the other

---

Case Study 10: Failed Secondary Rule - Emotional Learning

Market Context

This case study examines the psychological challenges when Secondary Rule application fails, demonstrating how proper mindset handles adverse outcomes.

Setup Analysis:

The Ultimate Stop-Loss

- **Pair:** EUR/CHF

- **Pattern:** Bearish engulfing at 0.9650

- **Primary Rule:** Stop at 0.9720 (70 pip distance)

- **Secondary Rule:** Stop at 0.9665 (15 pip distance)

Emotional Decision Making: Trader chose Secondary Rule not based on structural analysis, but because:

- Wanted larger position size

- Felt 70 pips was "too much risk"

- Recent wins created overconfidence

- Failed to follow decision matrix properly

Trade Execution:

- **Entry:** 0.9650

- **Stop:** 0.9665

- **Size:** 13.3 lots (oversized due to tight stop)

Rapid Stop-Out:

- **Day 1:** Price spikes to 0.9668, triggering stop

- **Loss:** $2,000 (full planned risk)

- **Time in trade:** 6 hours

Psychological Response Stages:

Stage 1: Denial

- "It was just a spike"

- "Market makers hunting stops"

- "Setup was still valid"

Stage 2: Anger

126

The Ultimate Stop-Loss

- Frustration with "unfair" price action

- Blame on external factors

- Desire for revenge trading

Stage 3: Bargaining

- "Should have used Primary Rule"

- "Maybe I can re-enter"

- "Next trade will make it back"

Stage 4: Depression

- Account balance focus

- Confidence shaken

- Trading paralysis

Stage 5: Acceptance

- Rule violation acknowledgment

- Learning opportunity recognition

- Commitment to proper methodology

Subsequent Price Action:

- **Day 2:** Price falls to 0.9635

- **Day 4:** Continues to 0.9590

- **Day 7:** Reaches 0.9550

Primary Rule Analysis: Had proper rule been followed:

- Stop at 0.9720 would not have been hit

- Position size: 2.86 lots (proper risk management)

- Profit achieved: 100+ pips = $2,860+

The Ultimate Stop-Loss

- Lesson: Methodology works when applied correctly

Emotional Learning Points:

1. **Rule violations carry double penalties:** Lost money AND missed opportunity

2. **Overconfidence creates poor decisions:** Recent success can lead to carelessness

3. **Emotional stages are normal:** Accepting the psychological process helps recovery

4. **Learning costs money:** Every violation teaches expensive but valuable lessons

5. **Methodology discipline:** Rules work when followed, fail when violated

Recovery Process:

- **Immediate:** No revenge trading, no position size increases

- **Short-term:** Return to paper trading to rebuild confidence

- **Medium-term:** Strict adherence to Primary Rule only

- **Long-term:** Gradual reintroduction of Secondary Rule with proper criteria

---

Psychological Patterns Across Case Studies

Pre-Trade Psychology:

Successful Trades:

- Calm, methodical analysis

- Clear rule selection reasoning

- Appropriate position sizing discipline

- Realistic profit expectations

The Ultimate Stop-Loss

Failed Trades:

- Rushed or emotional decision making

- Rule selection based on convenience

- Position sizing driven by greed or fear

- Unrealistic profit targeting

During-Trade Psychology:

Successful Management:

- Acceptance of planned risk

- Stop levels viewed as protection, not obstacles

- Focus on process rather than profit/loss

- Willingness to take partial profits

Failed Management:

- Constant stop level monitoring

- Emotional attachment to positions

- Focus on account balance changes

- All-or-nothing exit mentality

Post-Trade Psychology:

Constructive Processing:

- Analysis of what worked/didn't work

- Documentation of lessons learned

- Objective review of rule application

- Integration of experience into future trading

Destructive Processing:

The Ultimate Stop-Loss

- Blaming external factors for losses

- Overconfidence from profitable trades

- Failure to document decision processes

- Immediate jump to next trade without review

Building Your Psychological Framework

Daily Mental Preparation:

Pre-Market Routine:

1. **Review previous day's trades:** What worked? What didn't?

2. **Identify potential setups:** Which pairs showing engulfing potential?

3. **Confirm rule selection criteria:** Primary or Secondary Rule for each setup?

4. **Calculate position sizes:** Risk percentage and pip values ready

5. **Set psychological anchors:** Remind yourself why stops protect capital

During-Market Monitoring:

Emotional Check-ins:

- **Every 2 hours:** How are you feeling about open positions?

- **At stop approach:** Are you tempted to move stops? Why?

- **At profit target:** Are you being greedy or realistic?

- **During drawdowns:** Are you maintaining methodology discipline?

Post-Market Review:

Objective Assessment:

1. **Rule selection:** Was each choice structurally justified?

2. **Position sizing:** Did you maintain risk percentage discipline?

3. **Emotional states:** When did you feel most/least confident?

4. **Learning opportunities:** What will you do differently tomorrow?

Case Study Integration Exercise

Personal Development Task:

For each of the 10 case studies presented, complete this analysis:

Technical Analysis:

1. Do you agree with the rule selection? Why/why not?

2. Would you have calculated position size differently?

3. How would you have handled the trade management decisions?

Psychological Analysis:

1. Which case study scenarios would challenge your discipline most?

2. What emotional triggers do you recognize in yourself?

3. How would you prepare mentally for similar situations?

Risk Management Analysis:

1. Are the risk percentages appropriate for your account size?

2. How would correlation risk affect your trading?

3. What position sizing modifications would you make?

Integration Planning:

1. Which case study lessons apply most to your trading style?

2. What specific changes will you make to your methodology?

3. How will you measure improvement in these areas?

The Ultimate Stop-Loss

Advanced Case Study Applications

Multi-Setup Scenarios:

When multiple selling setups appear simultaneously:

Priority Matrix:

1. **Highest probability:** Best pattern quality + clearest structure

2. **Best risk-reward:** Optimal stop distance to profit target ratio

3. **Lowest correlation:** Minimize portfolio risk concentration

4. **Strongest confirmation:** Multiple timeframe agreement

Resource Allocation:

- **Never exceed total portfolio risk limits**

- **Consider execution timing and market sessions**

- **Account for spread and slippage on multiple positions**

- **Maintain reserve capital for additional opportunities**

Session-Specific Considerations:

Asian Session Selling:

- Lower volatility: Secondary Rule may be more appropriate

- Thinner liquidity: Widen buffers and reduce position sizes

- News events: Australian and Japanese data impacts

European Session Selling:

- Higher volatility: Primary Rule often more suitable

- Major pairs most active: Standard buffers typically adequate

- Central bank communications: Factor in policy announcement risks

The Ultimate Stop-Loss

US Session Selling:

- Peak volatility: Careful buffer calculations essential

- News-heavy environment: Consider event timing in rule selection

- Session overlap effects: London/New York overlap creates unique dynamics

Weekend Preparation:

Friday Close Checklist:

1. **Open position review:** Adequate protection for weekend gaps?

2. **News calendar check:** Weekend developments that could affect Monday open?

3. **Position sizing assessment:** Comfortable with gap risk on current size?

4. **Profit taking consideration:** Better to secure profits before weekend?

Mastery Development Progression

Beginner Stage (Months 1-3):

- Focus exclusively on Primary Rule

- Paper trade all setups for pattern recognition

- Document every decision and outcome

- Build confidence with smaller position sizes

Intermediate Stage (Months 4-9):

- Introduce Secondary Rule with strict criteria

- Begin real money trading with proven methodology

- Develop personal trade management style

- Handle first series of losses with discipline

Advanced Stage (Months 10+):

- Intuitive rule selection based on market structure

- Comfortable with full position sizing

- Adapt methodology for different market conditions

- Mentor others while continuing personal development

Mastery Indicators:

You've achieved selling setup mastery when:

- **Rule selection is automatic:** No hesitation between Primary/Secondary choices

- **Position sizing is intuitive:** Risk calculations become second nature

- **Emotional discipline is consistent:** Stops never moved, rules never violated

- **Trade management is strategic:** Profit taking and trailing based on structure

- **Learning never stops:** Each trade adds to methodology refinement

---

Chapter Summary: From Theory to Practice

These ten case studies represent the bridge between understanding selling rules and implementing them profitably in live markets. Each case offers specific lessons:

Technical Lessons:

- Primary Rule provides superior protection in most scenarios

- Secondary Rule works when structural criteria are met

- Market conditions require methodology adaptation

The Ultimate Stop-Loss

- Multiple timeframe confirmation improves outcomes

Risk Management Lessons:

- Position sizing discipline determines long-term success

- Correlation risk requires portfolio-level thinking

- Volatility adjustments protect capital during extreme conditions

- Weekend gaps and news events demand special consideration

Psychological Lessons:

- Emotional preparation prevents poor decisions

- Rule violations carry compounding penalties

- Learning from losses accelerates development

- Consistent methodology builds genuine confidence

Integration Lessons:

- Personal trading system must incorporate case study insights

- Documentation creates valuable feedback loops

- Continuous improvement requires honest self-assessment

- Mastery develops through disciplined repetition

Preparing for Advanced Applications

With selling methodology mastered through case study analysis, you're ready for Part Three's advanced applications:

- **Multiple Timeframe Confirmation:** Using weekly and monthly structure to enhance daily setups

- **News Event Navigation:** Trading through economic announcements and central bank communications

The Ultimate Stop-Loss

- **Scaling Strategies:** Building positions using proper stop placement methodology

- **Session-Specific Adaptations:** Optimizing for Asian, European, and US market characteristics

The case studies in this chapter provide the experiential foundation for these advanced concepts. Every scenario you've analyzed here will appear again in more complex forms as your trading evolves.

Remember: **Mastery isn't about perfection—it's about consistent application of proven methodology combined with continuous learning from real market experience.**

"The market is the ultimate teacher, but only for students who come prepared with proper methodology and the discipline to learn from every outcome." — **Royalty FX Academy Philosophy**

The Ultimate Stop-Loss

ENTRY

DB

BULLISH
ENGULFING

SL

Chapter 9: Multiple Timeframe Confirmation with Stops

"The timeframes may change, but the rules remain constant. Master traders see the forest and the trees simultaneously."

Introduction: The Power of Multiple Perspectives

When you master stop loss placement on a single timeframe, you've built a solid foundation. But the forex market operates simultaneously across multiple timeframes, each telling a piece of the same story. Chapter 9 will teach you how to apply your stop loss mastery across different timeframes while maintaining the integrity of our core rules.

The beauty of our system is its consistency—whether you're looking at a 1-hour chart or a daily chart, the principles of last low placement for buying and last high placement for selling remain unchanged. What changes is how we layer these timeframes for maximum confirmation and precision.

The Timeframe Hierarchy: Building Your Analysis Framework

The Three-Timeframe Approach

Professional traders use a systematic approach to timeframe analysis:

Higher Timeframe (HTF) - The Trend Identifier

- Daily or 4-Hour charts
- Determines overall market bias
- Identifies major support and resistance levels
- Shows the "big picture" trend direction

Entry Timeframe (ETF) - The Setup Spotter

- 1-Hour or 30-minute charts
- Where you identify specific entry setups

The Ultimate Stop-Loss

- Where you apply your bullish/bearish engulfing patterns

- The timeframe where you execute trades

Confirmation Timeframe (CTF) - The Precision Tool

- 15-minute or 5-minute charts

- Provides precise entry timing

- Confirms momentum and rejection patterns

- Fine-tunes your entry point

Stop Placement Across Timeframes: The Golden Rule

Here's the critical principle: **Your stop loss placement should always respect the timeframe where you identified your setup.**

If you spot a bullish engulfing pattern on the 1-hour chart, your stop goes at the last low on that same 1-hour chart—not the 15-minute or daily chart. This maintains consistency and ensures your risk management aligns with your analysis timeframe.

Practical Application: The Layered Analysis Process

Step 1: Higher Timeframe Bias Assessment

Begin with your higher timeframe to establish market context:

For Buying Setups:

- Is the daily/4H trend bullish?

- Are we above key moving averages?

- Is price respecting higher timeframe support levels?

- Where would the last low be placed on this timeframe?

For Selling Setups:

- Is the daily/4H trend bearish?

- Are we below key moving averages?

The Ultimate Stop-Loss

- Is price respecting higher timeframe resistance levels?

- Where would the last high be placed on this timeframe?

Step 2: Entry Timeframe Setup Identification

Move to your entry timeframe to find specific setups:

Buying Example - 1H Chart:

- Look for bullish engulfing patterns aligned with HTF bias

- Identify the last low for primary stop placement

- Check if a bullish engulfing low offers a tighter secondary stop option

- Ensure the setup respects higher timeframe structure

Selling Example - 1H Chart:

- Look for bearish engulfing patterns aligned with HTF bias

- Identify the last high for primary stop placement

- Check if a bearish engulfing high offers a tighter secondary stop option

- Ensure the setup respects higher timeframe structure

Step 3: Confirmation Timeframe Timing

Use your confirmation timeframe for precise entry:

- Look for momentum confirmation in your favor

- Watch for rejection patterns at key levels

- Time your entry for optimal risk-to-reward

- Confirm that lower timeframe action supports your higher timeframe bias

Real-World Example: EUR/USD Multi-Timeframe Analysis

Scenario: Bullish Setup Identification

Daily Chart Analysis (HTF):

The Ultimate Stop-Loss

- EUR/USD in clear uptrend above 200 EMA

- Recently bounced from major support level

- Last low on daily chart at 1.0850 (wide stop reference)

- Overall bias: BULLISH

1-Hour Chart Analysis (ETF):

- Bullish engulfing pattern formed at 1.0920 level

- Last low on 1H chart at 1.0895 (primary stop placement)

- Bullish engulfing low at 1.0915 (secondary stop option)

- Setup aligns with daily uptrend bias

15-Minute Chart Analysis (CTF):

- Strong rejection from 1.0915 level

- Momentum indicators turning bullish

- Entry timing confirmed at 1.0925 break

Trade Execution:

- Entry: 1.0925

- Primary Stop: 1.0895 (1H last low)

- Secondary Stop Option: 1.0915 (bullish engulfing low)

- Risk: 30 pips (using primary) or 10 pips (using secondary)

The Timeframe Conflict Resolution

When Timeframes Disagree

Sometimes different timeframes will show conflicting signals. Here's how to handle these situations:

HTF Bearish, ETF Bullish:

- Approach with extreme caution

The Ultimate Stop-Loss

- Consider smaller position sizes

- Look for higher timeframe support/resistance confluence

- May indicate a counter-trend bounce rather than trend change

HTF Bullish, ETF Bearish:

- May represent a healthy pullback in an uptrend

- Look for buying opportunities at higher timeframe support

- Wait for ETF to align with HTF bias

- Exercise patience for proper setup alignment

The Waiting Game: When Not to Trade

Master traders know when NOT to trade:

- When timeframes show complete contradiction

- When higher timeframe trend is unclear

- When approaching major news events

- When your setup timeframe shows indecision

Advanced Concepts: Multiple Setup Confirmation

Stacked Setups

The most powerful trades occur when multiple timeframes show similar setups:

Example: Triple Confluence Buying

- Daily chart shows bullish engulfing at major support

- 4H chart shows bullish engulfing at trend line

- 1H chart shows bullish engulfing at previous resistance turned support

In such cases, use the entry timeframe (1H) for stop placement while recognizing the exceptional strength of the setup.

The Ultimate Stop-Loss

Nested Stop Levels

Advanced traders identify multiple stop levels across timeframes:

Buying Example:

- Daily last low: 1.0800 (ultimate disaster stop)

- 4H last low: 1.0850 (swing stop)

- 1H last low: 1.0890 (active trading stop)

Start with the 1H stop (following our rules) but be aware of these nested levels for position management decisions.

Position Sizing Across Timeframes

Risk Adjustment for Timeframe Selection

Different timeframes require different position sizing approaches:

Higher Timeframe Stops (Wider):

- Require smaller position sizes

- Offer better risk-to-reward potential

- Suit swing trading approaches

- Need more patience for development

Lower Timeframe Stops (Tighter):

- Allow larger position sizes

- May offer quicker profits

- Suit scalping/day trading

- Require more active monitoring

The 1% Rule Application

Regardless of timeframe, maintain consistent risk percentage:

- 1% account risk per trade

The Ultimate Stop-Loss

- Adjust position size based on stop distance

- Calculate: Position Size = (Account Risk ÷ Stop Distance) × 100,000

Common Multiple Timeframe Mistakes

Mistake #1: Stop Placement Confusion

Wrong: Using daily chart setup with 15-minute stop placement **Right:** Matching stop timeframe to setup timeframe

Mistake #2: Analysis Paralysis

Wrong: Analyzing 7+ timeframes before making a decision **Right:** Stick to your 3-timeframe system (HTF, ETF, CTF)

Mistake #3: Timeframe Shopping

Wrong: Switching timeframes until you find a bullish signal **Right:** Objective analysis starting from higher timeframe down

Mistake #4: Ignoring Higher Timeframe Context

Wrong: Taking counter-trend trades without HTF awareness **Right:** Always respecting the higher timeframe bias

Practice Exercises: Multiple Timeframe Mastery

Exercise 1: Timeframe Hierarchy Setup

1. Choose a currency pair

2. Identify your three timeframes (HTF, ETF, CTF)

3. Analyze each timeframe following the process outlined

4. Document your bias, setup, and stop placement reasoning

Exercise 2: Conflict Resolution Practice

1. Find examples where HTF and ETF show conflicting signals

2. Document your decision-making process

3. Note whether you would trade or wait

4. Review outcomes to refine your approach

Exercise 3: Stop Level Mapping

1. Identify nested stop levels across multiple timeframes

2. Calculate position sizes for each stop level option

3. Determine which approach best fits your risk tolerance

4. Practice this analysis on historical charts

Chapter 9 Summary: Timeframe Mastery Keys

Multiple timeframe analysis enhances your stop loss mastery without changing the fundamental rules:

1. **Consistency is King:** Stop placement rules remain the same across all timeframes

2. **Hierarchy Matters:** Higher timeframe provides context, entry timeframe provides setup

3. **Alignment is Power:** The strongest trades show timeframe confluence

4. **Patience Pays:** Wait for proper timeframe alignment rather than forcing trades

5. **Risk Management:** Adjust position sizes based on timeframe-specific stop distances

Your stop loss placement becomes even more powerful when supported by multiple timeframe confirmation. The rules remain simple—only the context becomes richer.

The Ultimate Stop-Loss

Chapter 10: News Events and Market Sessions

"The market's heartbeat changes with the news and sessions. Master traders adapt their stops to the market's rhythm while maintaining their core principles."

Introduction: Trading in the Real World

The forex market never sleeps, but its personality changes dramatically throughout the day. From the quiet Asian session to the volatile London-New York overlap, each period brings unique characteristics that affect how you should approach stop loss placement.

Similarly, news events can transform a calm market into a raging storm within seconds. Chapter 10 will teach you how to maintain your stop loss mastery while adapting to these market realities.

The core principle remains unchanged: your stops go at the last low when buying and last high when selling. What changes is your awareness of when these levels might be more or less reliable based on market conditions.

Understanding Market Sessions: The Forex Day Cycle

The Three Major Sessions

Asian Session (Tokyo) - The Foundation Builder

- Time: 11:00 PM - 8:00 AM GMT

- Characteristics: Lower volatility, range-bound movement

- Major pairs: JPY crosses most active

- Stop Considerations: More reliable in trending conditions, prone to false breakouts

European Session (London) - The Trend Maker

- Time: 7:00 AM - 4:00 PM GMT

- Characteristics: High volatility, strong trends

The Ultimate Stop-Loss

- Major pairs: EUR, GBP pairs most active

- Stop Considerations: Strong momentum can invalidate nearby stops quickly

American Session (New York) - The Trend Confirmer

- Time: 12:00 PM - 9:00 PM GMT

- Characteristics: High volatility, trend continuation or reversal

- Major pairs: USD pairs dominate

- Stop Considerations: Institutional flows can cause sudden moves

Session Overlap Periods: Maximum Opportunity and Risk

London-New York Overlap (12:00 PM - 4:00 PM GMT):

- Highest volatility period

- Maximum liquidity

- Strongest trend moves

- Most reliable stop levels due to high participation

Asian-European Overlap (7:00 AM - 8:00 AM GMT):

- Moderate volatility increase

- European traders react to Asian developments

- Can see breakouts from Asian ranges

Stop Loss Adaptation by Session

Asian Session Stop Strategy

Characteristics:

- Lower volatility means tighter ranges

- Less likely to see dramatic stop runs

- Range-bound conditions more common

The Ultimate Stop-Loss

Stop Placement Adaptations:

- Standard rules apply but with extra caution on breakouts

- Look for multiple touches of support/resistance before trusting levels

- Consider waiting for European session confirmation on breakout trades

Example: USD/JPY in Asian Session

- Bullish engulfing forms at 149.20 during Tokyo hours

- Last low at 148.95 (25-pip stop)

- Asian session reliability: Moderate - watch for European confirmation

European Session Stop Strategy

Characteristics:

- High volatility from session start

- Strong trending moves

- Economic data releases common

Stop Placement Adaptations:

- Wider stops may be necessary due to increased volatility

- News events can cause gap movements past stops

- Strong institutional participation makes levels more reliable

Example: EUR/USD in London Session

- Bearish engulfing forms at 1.0950 during London open

- Last high at 1.0975 (25-pip stop)

- European session reliability: High - strong momentum likely

American Session Stop Strategy

The Ultimate Stop-Loss

Characteristics:

- Continuation of European trends or major reversals

- US economic data impact

- End-of-day institutional flows

Stop Placement Adaptations:

- Watch for trend exhaustion signals

- Friday afternoon can see profit-taking moves

- Month-end/quarter-end flows can distort normal patterns

Example: GBP/USD in New York Session

- Bullish engulfing forms at 1.2650 during NY morning

- Last low at 1.2625 (25-pip stop)

- American session reliability: High - good follow-through potential

News Events: Navigating Market Storms

High-Impact News Categories

Central Bank Decisions:

- Interest rate announcements

- Monetary policy statements

- Governor/Chairman speeches

- Minutes from policy meetings

Economic Indicators:

- Employment data (NFP, unemployment rates)

- Inflation data (CPI, PPI)

- GDP releases

- Manufacturing/services PMI

Geopolitical Events:

- Election results

- Trade negotiations

- Conflict developments

- Regulatory changes

Pre-News Stop Management

The 30-Minute Rule: Stop taking new positions 30 minutes before high-impact news releases. This prevents getting caught in pre-news positioning or gap movements.

Existing Position Management:

- **Option 1:** Close positions before news if uncertain about outcome

- **Option 2:** Move stops to breakeven if in profit

- **Option 3:** Maintain positions if news aligns with your bias and you accept the risk

Stop Placement Considerations Before News:

- Widen stops slightly to account for increased volatility

- Place stops beyond obvious technical levels that might get hit during news spikes

- Consider the currency involved - USD news affects all USD pairs

Post-News Stop Strategies

Immediate Post-News (0-15 minutes):

- Avoid new trades during initial volatility spike

- Let dust settle before assessing new opportunities

- Existing stops should remain in place unless hit

The Ultimate Stop-Loss

Settling Period (15-60 minutes):

- Look for new setups that incorporate news-driven moves

- Apply standard stop rules to any new patterns

- Assess whether news changed overall market structure

New Normal (1+ hours post-news):

- Resume normal trading operations

- Incorporate any new support/resistance levels created by news moves

- Update your bias if fundamentals have shifted

Session-Specific Setup Examples

Asian Session Setup: USD/JPY Range Trading

Market Context:

- Tokyo session, low volatility expected

- USD/JPY in 149.00-149.50 range for past week

- No major news expected

Setup Identification:

- Bullish engulfing forms at 149.05 (near range bottom)

- Last low at 148.90 (15-pip stop)

- Range top target at 149.45 (40-pip profit potential)

Session-Specific Considerations:

- Asian session ranges often hold

- Risk-to-reward looks attractive (1:2.6)

- Plan to close before London open if not moving

The Ultimate Stop-Loss

European Session Setup: EUR/USD Trend Continuation

Market Context:

- London session open, ECB press conference in 2 hours

- EUR/USD in strong uptrend, pullback complete

- High volatility expected

Setup Identification:

- Bullish engulfing at 1.0920 (trend line support)

- Last low at 1.0895 (25-pip stop)

- Trend continuation target at 1.0980 (60-pip profit potential)

Session-Specific Considerations:

- European session momentum supports setup

- Wide stop appropriate for session volatility

- Monitor ECB news for continued validity

American Session Setup: GBP/USD Reversal Play

Market Context:

- New York session, US employment data just released (positive)

- GBP/USD rejected from major resistance

- High volatility, potential trend change

Setup Identification:

- Bearish engulfing at 1.2750 (major resistance)

- Last high at 1.2770 (20-pip stop)

- Support target at 1.2680 (70-pip profit potential)

The Ultimate Stop-Loss

Session-Specific Considerations:

- US data supports USD strength

- American session follow-through likely

- Wide profit target appropriate for session volatility

News Event Case Study: Non-Farm Payrolls (NFP)

Pre-NFP Preparation (Day Before)

Market Analysis:

- USD pairs showing mixed signals

- Employment trend has been strong

- Market expects +200K jobs added

Position Management:

- Close any USD scalping positions

- Keep swing trades with wide stops (beyond typical NFP spike range)

- Prepare for post-NFP opportunities

NFP Release Day Strategy

2 Hours Before (6:30 AM EST):

- Final position review

- No new trades until after release

- Identify key levels for post-NFP analysis

30 Minutes Before (8:00 AM EST):

- Complete trading halt

- Monitor for any early leaks or positioning

Release Time (8:30 AM EST):

The Ultimate Stop-Loss

- Observe market reaction

- Note initial direction and magnitude

- Wait for settling before analysis

Post-NFP Analysis (9:00 AM EST onwards):

- Assess new market structure

- Look for setups that incorporate NFP move

- Apply standard stop rules to new patterns

Post-NFP Setup Example

Scenario: NFP beats expectations significantly, USD surges

EUR/USD Response:

- Drops from 1.0950 to 1.0890 in 15 minutes

- Finds support at 1.0885 (previous resistance)

- Forms potential double bottom pattern

New Setup Identification:

- Bullish engulfing forms at 1.0890 (support test)

- Last low at 1.0875 (15-pip stop)

- Retracement target at 1.0920 (30-pip profit potential)

Post-News Considerations:

- Tight stop appropriate as major volatility passed

- Good risk-to-reward setup

- USD strength may limit upside, so take profits quickly

Session Transition Strategies

Asian to European Transition

The Ultimate Stop-Loss

Common Patterns:

- Asian range breakouts during European open

- Trend continuation from previous day's European session

- Gap fills from overnight news

Stop Management:

- Tighten stops on Asian range trades before European open

- Prepare for increased volatility

- Look for continuation or reversal setups

European to American Transition

Common Patterns:

- Trend acceleration during overlap period

- US data reaction overlaid on European moves

- Institutional rebalancing flows

Stop Management:

- Maintain stops during overlap period

- Watch for trend exhaustion signals

- Prepare for end-of-day flows

Weekend and Holiday Considerations

Weekend Gap Management

Friday Close Strategy:

- Consider closing positions before weekend

- If holding, ensure stops are beyond typical gap ranges

- Review upcoming weekend news events

The Ultimate Stop-Loss

Monday Open Strategy:

- Assess gap direction and magnitude
- Look for gap fill opportunities
- Apply standard stop rules to new setups

Holiday Trading

Reduced Liquidity Periods:

- Christmas/New Year period
- Summer holidays (August)
- Local holidays in major financial centers

Adaptations:

- Wider stops to account for thin liquidity
- Smaller position sizes
- Increased caution on breakout trades

Risk Management During High Volatility

Position Sizing Adjustments

High Volatility Sessions:

- Reduce position sizes by 25-50%
- Account for wider stop requirements
- Maintain same percentage risk per trade

Low Volatility Sessions:

- Can use standard position sizes
- Tighter stops may allow larger positions

- Watch for false breakouts

Multiple Position Management

Session Overlap Periods:

- Limit number of simultaneous positions

- Ensure positions aren't highly correlated

- Monitor total account exposure

News Event Periods:

- Consider closing correlated positions

- Reduce overall exposure before major announcements

- Plan post-news re-entry strategy

Technology and News Trading

Economic Calendar Usage

Essential Information:

- Impact level (High/Medium/Low)

- Previous/Forecast/Actual values

- Time of release

- Currency affected

Pre-Planning:

- Mark high-impact events on charts

- Set alerts for major releases

- Prepare multiple scenarios

News Feed Integration

Real-Time Monitoring:

The Ultimate Stop-Loss

- Professional news services

- Central bank feeds

- Social media monitoring

Reaction Speed:

- Don't chase immediate moves

- Wait for confirmation

- Stick to your systematic approach

Chapter 10 Summary: Session and News Mastery

Trading successfully across different sessions and news events requires adaptability while maintaining core principles:

1. **Session Awareness:** Each session has unique characteristics that affect stop reliability

2. **News Preparation:** Plan ahead for high-impact events and adjust risk accordingly

3. **Volatility Adaptation:** Adjust position sizes and stop placement for market conditions

4. **Patience During Chaos:** Avoid trading during maximum uncertainty periods

5. **Core Rules Remain:** Last low/high placement principles apply across all conditions

The market's rhythm changes, but your discipline and systematic approach to stops should remain constant. Master traders adapt their tactics while preserving their strategic principles.

Understanding when and how to trade different sessions and navigate news events will elevate your stop loss mastery from mechanical rule-following to dynamic market adaptation. The strongest traders are those who can maintain their edge across all market conditions.

The Ultimate Stop-Loss

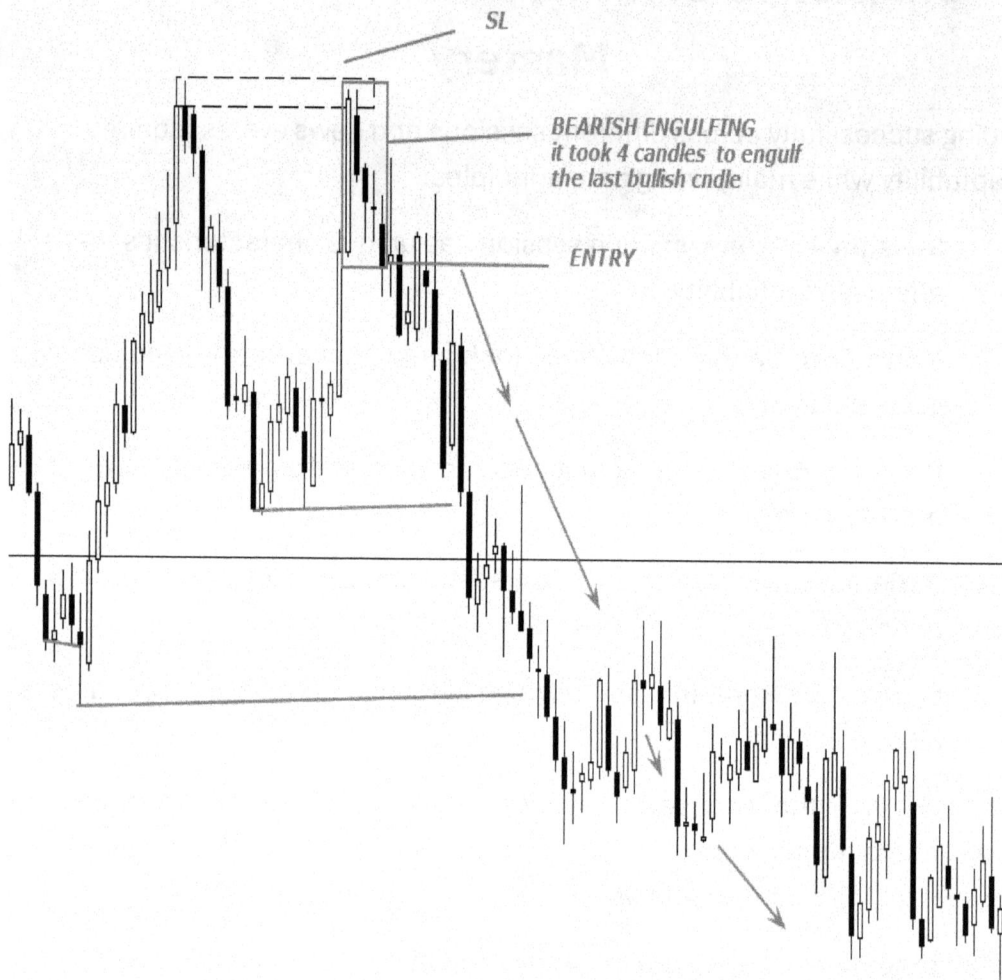

SL

BEARISH ENGULFING
*it took 4 candles to engulf
the last bullish cndle*

ENTRY

The Ultimate Stop-Loss

Chapter 11: Scaling Strategies with Proper Stops

"A master builder doesn't construct the entire house at once. Position scaling with proper stops is the art of building wealth one calculated brick at a time."

Introduction: The Art of Strategic Position Building

Most traders think in terms of single entries and exits—one trade, one stop, one outcome. But professional traders understand that the biggest profits often come from building positions methodically over time. This is called scaling or pyramiding.

Chapter 11 will teach you how to apply your stop loss mastery to scaling strategies, maintaining proper risk management while maximizing profit potential from strong trending moves.

The fundamental principle remains unchanged: each position in your scale must have proper stop placement following our core rules. What changes is how you coordinate multiple positions to create a larger, more profitable overall trade.

Understanding Position Scaling: The Foundation

What is Position Scaling?

Position scaling involves adding to a winning trade as it moves in your favor. Instead of taking one large position, you build it gradually, using the market's confirmation of your analysis to justify increased exposure.

Traditional Single Entry:

- Enter 1.00 lot at 1.0900

- Stop at 1.0875 (25 pips)

- Risk: $250 (assuming $10/pip)

Scaled Entry Example:

- Entry 1: 0.50 lot at 1.0900, stop at 1.0875

- Entry 2: 0.30 lot at 1.0925, stop at 1.0900 (breakeven of Entry 1)

The Ultimate Stop-Loss

- Entry 3: 0.20 lot at 1.0950, stop at 1.0925 (breakeven of Entry 2)

- Total: 1.00 lot with improved average entry and reduced risk

The Psychology of Scaling

Benefits:

- Reduces impact of poor timing on single large entry

- Allows you to increase position size as trade proves correct

- Provides multiple opportunities to enter trending moves

- Psychologically easier than risking large amounts immediately

Challenges:

- Requires discipline to add to winners (counter-intuitive)

- More complex position management

- Can reduce profit if trend reverses quickly

- Requires clear rules to avoid over-leveraging

The Scaling Framework: Rules and Structure

Rule #1: Only Scale Into Winners

Never add to losing positions (averaging down). This violates fundamental risk management principles and can turn small losses into account-destroying disasters.

Correct Scaling:

- Price moves in your favor before adding

- Each new position has its own stop loss

- Overall position risk remains controlled

Incorrect Scaling (Never Do This):

- Adding to losing trades hoping for recovery

- Moving stops further away to accommodate new positions

- Ignoring overall account risk limits

Rule #2: Each Position Follows Stop Loss Rules

Every position in your scale must follow the primary and secondary stop placement rules established in earlier chapters.

For Buying Scales:

- Primary Rule: Stop at last low of entry timeframe

- Secondary Rule: Stop at bullish engulfing low if applicable

- Each new position gets its own stop analysis

For Selling Scales:

- Primary Rule: Stop at last high of entry timeframe

- Secondary Rule: Stop at bearish engulfing high if applicable

- Each new position gets its own stop analysis

Rule #3: Progressive Stop Management

As you add positions, earlier stops should be moved to protect profits while new positions maintain their technical stops.

Stop Evolution Pattern:

- Position 1: Technical stop (last low/high)

- Position 2: Move Position 1 stop to breakeven, set Position 2 technical stop

- Position 3: Move Position 2 stop to breakeven, set Position 3 technical stop

- Continue pattern for additional positions

The Ultimate Stop-Loss

Scaling Entry Strategies

The Breakout Scaling Method

Best used when a strong trend breaks through significant resistance/support levels.

Buying Example: EUR/USD Uptrend Breakout

Position 1 - Initial Breakout:

- Entry: 1.0950 (break above 1.0945 resistance)
- Size: 0.4 lots
- Stop: 1.0925 (last low, 25 pips)
- Risk: $100

Position 2 - Momentum Confirmation:

- Entry: 1.0975 (after pullback and bounce from 1.0950)
- Size: 0.3 lots
- Stop: 1.0950 (breakeven of Position 1)
- Position 1 Stop: Moved to 1.0950 (breakeven)
- Additional Risk: $75

Position 3 - Trend Extension:

- Entry: 1.1000 (break above 1.0995 minor resistance)
- Size: 0.3 lots
- Stop: 1.0975 (breakeven of Position 2)
- Position 2 Stop: Moved to 1.0975 (breakeven)
- Additional Risk: $75

Total Position: 1.0 lots with average entry of 1.0970, maximum risk of $250, but current risk much lower due to breakeven stops.

The Ultimate Stop-Loss

The Pullback Scaling Method

Used when trending markets provide multiple retracement opportunities.

Selling Example: GBP/USD Downtrend Pullbacks

Position 1 - First Pullback:

- Entry: 1.2750 (bearish engulfing at resistance)

- Size: 0.5 lots

- Stop: 1.2775 (last high, 25 pips)

- Risk: $125

Position 2 - Second Pullback:

- Entry: 1.2720 (bearish engulfing at lower resistance)

- Size: 0.3 lots

- Stop: 1.2745 (last high for this entry)

- Position 1 Stop: Moved to 1.2745 (profit protection)

- Additional Risk: $75

Position 3 - Third Pullback:

- Entry: 1.2690 (bearish engulfing at trend line)

- Size: 0.2 lots

- Stop: 1.2715 (last high for this entry)

- Position 2 Stop: Moved to 1.2715 (profit protection)

- Additional Risk: $50

Total Position: 1.0 lots with average entry of 1.2730, protected by progressive stops.

The Support/Resistance Scaling Method

The Ultimate Stop-Loss

Adds positions at multiple support levels (for buying) or resistance levels (for selling).

Buying Example: USD/JPY Support Zone Scaling

Market Context:

- USD/JPY in uptrend
- Multiple support levels identified: 149.00, 148.75, 148.50
- Plan to scale at each level if tested

Position 1 - First Support Test:

- Entry: 149.05 (bullish engulfing at 149.00 support)
- Size: 0.3 lots
- Stop: 148.85 (below support zone, 20 pips)
- Risk: $60

Position 2 - Deeper Support Test:

- Entry: 148.80 (bullish engulfing at 148.75 support)
- Size: 0.4 lots
- Stop: 148.60 (below deeper support, 20 pips)
- Position 1 Stop: Moved to 148.90 (reduce risk)
- Additional Risk: $80

Position 3 - Final Support Test:

- Entry: 148.55 (bullish engulfing at 148.50 support)
- Size: 0.3 lots
- Stop: 148.35 (below final support, 20 pips)
- Earlier stops: Moved to protect profits
- Additional Risk: $60

The Ultimate Stop-Loss

Advanced Scaling Concepts

The Pyramid Scaling Model

Position sizes decrease as you add to the trade, creating a pyramid shape.

Structure:

- Position 1: Largest size (base of pyramid)

- Position 2: Medium size

- Position 3: Smallest size (top of pyramid)

Benefits:

- Largest position gets best entry price

- Reduced risk as trade develops

- Maintains good average entry price

Example Pyramid:

- Position 1: 0.5 lots

- Position 2: 0.3 lots

- Position 3: 0.2 lots

- Total: 1.0 lots

The Equal Weight Scaling Model

All positions are the same size for simplicity.

Structure:

- Position 1: 0.33 lots

- Position 2: 0.33 lots

- Position 3: 0.34 lots

- Total: 1.0 lots

The Ultimate Stop-Loss

Benefits:

- Simple to manage and calculate

- Equal risk per entry

- Good for systematic approaches

The Accelerated Scaling Model

Position sizes increase with each addition (inverse pyramid).

When to Use:

- Only in very strong trending conditions

- When conviction increases with each confirmation

- Requires strict risk management discipline

Caution: This method increases risk significantly and should only be used by experienced traders in exceptional circumstances.

Risk Management in Scaling

The 1% Rule Applied to Scaling

Your total scaled position should not risk more than your normal single-trade risk.

Example Calculation:

- Account Size: $10,000

- Maximum Risk: 1% = $100

- Plan: 3-position scale

Position Sizing:

- Position 1: Risk $40 (0.4% of account)

- Position 2: Risk $35 (0.35% of account)

- Position 3: Risk $25 (0.25% of account)

The Ultimate Stop-Loss

- Total Risk: $100 (1% of account)

Stop Loss Coordination

Managing multiple stops requires systematic approach:

Stop Types in Scaling:

1. **Technical Stops:** Based on chart analysis (our primary rules)

2. **Breakeven Stops:** Protect earlier positions from loss

3. **Trailing Stops:** Lock in profits as trade develops

4. **Time Stops:** Exit if trend stalls too long

Stop Management Sequence:

1. Enter Position 1 with technical stop

2. When adding Position 2, move Position 1 to breakeven

3. When adding Position 3, move Position 2 to breakeven

4. Trail all stops as trend continues

Maximum Position Limits

Set clear limits to prevent over-scaling:

Account-Based Limits:

- Maximum 3% total account risk across all positions

- No more than 5 positions in any single pair

- Maximum total position size: 3x your normal trade size

Time-Based Limits:

- Complete scaling within 4 hours for day trades

- Complete scaling within 3 days for swing trades

- Exit all positions if trend stalls for predetermined time

The Ultimate Stop-Loss

Scaling Exit Strategies

The Partial Profit Method

Close portions of your scaled position at different profit targets.

Example Structure:

- Close 1/3 at first resistance level

- Close 1/3 at second resistance level

- Trail stop on final 1/3 for maximum profit

Benefits:

- Guarantees some profit taking

- Allows participation in extended moves

- Reduces regret from early/late exits

The All-or-Nothing Method

Hold entire scaled position until single exit signal.

When to Use:

- Very strong trending conditions

- Clear trend-following system signals

- High conviction trades only

Exit Signals:

- Major trend line break

- Key support/resistance level failure

- Momentum divergence confirmation

- Time-based exit rules

The Trailing Stop Method

The Ultimate Stop-Loss

Use systematic trailing stops to lock in profits while allowing for trend continuation.

Trailing Options:

- ATR-based trails (2x Average True Range)

- Percentage trails (2-3% from highs/lows)

- Technical level trails (moving averages, trend lines)

- Time-decay trails (tighten over time)

Technology and Scaling

Position Management Tools

Trade Journals for Scaling:

- Track each position separately

- Monitor overall risk exposure

- Record scaling decisions and outcomes

- Analyze scaling effectiveness

Platform Features:

- Multiple position capability

- Automated stop management

- Risk calculation tools

- Position sizing calculators

Alert Systems for Scaling

Entry Alerts:

- Price alerts for additional scaling levels

- Technical pattern completion alerts

- Support/resistance test notifications

The Ultimate Stop-Loss

Management Alerts:

- Stop loss hit notifications

- Profit target reached alerts

- Time-based review reminders

Common Scaling Mistakes

Mistake #1: Scaling Into Losers

Wrong: Adding to losing positions hoping for recovery **Right:** Only scale into profitable positions

Mistake #2: Ignoring Overall Risk

Wrong: Each position risks 1%, total risk becomes 3%+ **Right:** Total scaled position risks your normal amount (1%)

Mistake #3: No Clear Exit Plan

Wrong: Adding positions without knowing how you'll exit **Right:** Plan entire scaling sequence before first entry

Mistake #4: Emotional Scaling

Wrong: Adding positions based on hope or fear **Right:** Systematic scaling based on predetermined rules

Mistake #5: Over-Complicating

Wrong: Managing 7+ positions simultaneously **Right:** Limit scaling to 3-4 positions maximum

Scaling Practice Exercises

Exercise 1: Paper Trade Scaling

1. Identify a trending market

2. Plan a 3-position scale

3. Execute on paper/demo account

4. Track results and decision quality

Exercise 2: Historical Analysis

1. Find past trending moves on charts

2. Identify optimal scaling entry points

3. Calculate what results would have been

4. Compare to single entry/exit approach

Exercise 3: Risk Calculation Practice

1. Choose account size and risk percentage

2. Plan scaling sequence with position sizes

3. Calculate stops and total risk

4. Ensure compliance with risk management rules

Real-World Scaling Case Study: EUR/USD Uptrend

Market Setup

- EUR/USD breaks above major resistance at 1.0850

- Clear uptrend established on daily chart

- Plan: 3-position scale on pullbacks

Position 1: Initial Breakout

- **Date:** Monday 9:00 AM London

- **Entry:** 1.0855 (break above 1.0850 resistance)

- **Size:** 0.4 lots ($4/pip)

- **Stop:** 1.0825 (last low, 30 pips)

- **Risk:** $120

- **Rationale:** Strong breakout with volume

The Ultimate Stop-Loss

Position 2: Pullback Entry

- **Date:** Tuesday 2:00 PM London

- **Entry:** 1.0885 (bullish engulfing at pullback)

- **Size:** 0.3 lots ($3/pip)

- **Stop:** 1.0860 (last low for this timeframe, 25 pips)

- **Additional Risk:** $75

- **Position 1 Stop:** Moved to 1.0860 (reduce risk)

- **Rationale:** Healthy pullback, good entry point

Position 3: Trend Continuation

- **Date:** Wednesday 10:00 AM London

- **Entry:** 1.0915 (break above minor resistance)

- **Size:** 0.3 lots ($3/pip)

- **Stop:** 1.0890 (last low, 25 pips)

- **Additional Risk:** $75

- **Earlier Stops:** Moved to protect profits

- **Rationale:** Continued strength, final position

Exit Strategy

- **Target 1:** 1.0950 (close 1/3 of total position)

- **Target 2:** 1.0980 (close 1/3 of total position)

- **Final:** Trail stop on remaining 1/3

Results Analysis

- **Total Position:** 1.0 lots

- **Average Entry:** 1.0880

The Ultimate Stop-Loss

- **Maximum Risk:** $270 (reduced to ~$100 after stop moves)

- **Profit at Target 2:** +$950

- **Risk-Reward:** Exceptional due to scaling efficiency

Chapter 11 Summary: Scaling Mastery Keys

Position scaling amplifies the power of your stop loss mastery:

1. **Scale Only Winners:** Never add to losing positions

2. **Each Position Follows Rules:** Apply stop placement rules to every entry

3. **Progressive Risk Management:** Move earlier stops as you add positions

4. **Maintain Overall Risk Limits:** Total scaled position shouldn't exceed normal risk

5. **Plan Complete Strategy:** Know your exits before making first entry

6. **Start Simple:** Begin with 2-3 position scales before attempting complex strategies

Scaling transforms good trades into great trades by allowing you to build larger positions while maintaining proper risk management. The key is applying your stop loss mastery systematically across multiple positions while keeping the big picture in focus.

Master traders understand that the biggest profits come not from perfect timing, but from staying with winning trades longer and building positions methodically. Scaling with proper stops is your tool for capturing these larger moves while protecting your capital.

The Ultimate Stop-Loss

Chapter 12: Position Sizing Calculator and Formulas

"Position sizing is where mathematics meets psychology. Get the formula right, and your emotions will follow."

Introduction: The Mathematics of Success

You've mastered stop loss placement using the last low and last high principles. You understand market sessions, news events, and scaling strategies. But without proper position sizing, even perfect stop placement becomes meaningless.

Chapter 12 will provide you with the mathematical foundation to calculate exact position sizes for any trade setup. These formulas ensure that every trade you take aligns with your risk management rules, regardless of stop distance or currency pair.

The goal is simple: risk the same percentage of your account on every trade while adapting position size to accommodate different stop loss distances. Master these calculations, and you'll trade with the confidence that comes from mathematical precision.

The Foundation Formula: Risk-Based Position Sizing

The Core Equation

Every position size calculation starts with this fundamental formula:

Position Size = (Account Risk ÷ Stop Loss Distance) × Contract Size

Where:

- **Account Risk** = Your predetermined risk amount in account currency

- **Stop Loss Distance** = Distance from entry to stop in pips

- **Contract Size** = Standard lot size (100,000 units) or mini lot (10,000 units)

The Ultimate Stop-Loss

Breaking Down the Components

Account Risk Calculation:

- Account Balance × Risk Percentage = Account Risk

- Example: $10,000 × 1% = $100 risk per trade

Stop Loss Distance:

- Entry Price - Stop Loss Price = Stop Distance (for buying)

- Stop Loss Price - Entry Price = Stop Distance (for selling)

- Convert to pips by moving decimal places based on currency pair

Contract Size Considerations:

- Standard Lot: 100,000 units

- Mini Lot: 10,000 units

- Micro Lot: 1,000 units

Practical Position Sizing Examples

Example 1: EUR/USD Buy Setup

Trade Setup:

- Account Balance: $10,000

- Risk Percentage: 1%

- Entry Price: 1.0950

- Stop Loss: 1.0925 (last low)

- Stop Distance: 25 pips

Calculation Steps:

Step 1: Calculate Account Risk Account Risk = $10,000 × 1% = $100

Step 2: Calculate Pip Value For EUR/USD (quote currency = USD):

The Ultimate Stop-Loss

- Standard Lot Pip Value = $10 per pip

- Mini Lot Pip Value = $1 per pip

Step 3: Calculate Position Size Position Size = Account Risk ÷ (Stop Distance × Pip Value) Position Size = $100 ÷ (25 pips × $1) Position Size = $100 ÷ $25 = 4 mini lots (0.4 standard lots)

Trade Summary:

- Position: 0.4 lots

- Risk: $100 (1% of account)

- Stop Distance: 25 pips

- If stopped out: Lose exactly $100

Example 2: GBP/JPY Sell Setup

Trade Setup:

- Account Balance: $25,000

- Risk Percentage: 1%

- Entry Price: 185.50

- Stop Loss: 186.00 (last high)

- Stop Distance: 50 pips

Calculation Steps:

Step 1: Calculate Account Risk Account Risk = $25,000 × 1% = $250

Step 2: Calculate Pip Value for GBP/JPY GBP/JPY pip value depends on current USD/JPY rate If USD/JPY = 150.00: Standard Lot Pip Value = (0.01 ÷ 150.00) × 100,000 = $6.67 per pip

Step 3: Calculate Position Size Position Size = $250 ÷ (50 pips × $6.67) Position Size = $250 ÷ $333.50 = 0.75 standard lots

Trade Summary:

The Ultimate Stop-Loss

- Position: 0.75 lots

- Risk: $250 (1% of account)

- Stop Distance: 50 pips

- If stopped out: Lose exactly $250

Example 3: USD/CAD Buy Setup

Trade Setup:

- Account Balance: $50,000

- Risk Percentage: 0.5% (conservative approach)

- Entry Price: 1.3650

- Stop Loss: 1.3620 (last low)

- Stop Distance: 30 pips

Calculation Steps:

Step 1: Calculate Account Risk Account Risk = $50,000 × 0.5% = $250

Step 2: Calculate Pip Value for USD/CAD For USD/CAD (base currency = USD): Standard Lot Pip Value = $10 ÷ 1.3650 = $7.33 per pip

Step 3: Calculate Position Size Position Size = $250 ÷ (30 pips × $7.33) Position Size = $250 ÷ $219.90 = 1.14 standard lots

Trade Summary:

- Position: 1.14 lots

- Risk: $250 (0.5% of account)

- Stop Distance: 30 pips

- If stopped out: Lose exactly $250

Advanced Position Sizing Formulas

The Universal Pip Value Calculator

The Ultimate Stop-Loss

For any currency pair, calculate pip value using this formula:

Pip Value = (Pip Size × Position Size) ÷ Exchange Rate

Where:

- Pip Size = 0.0001 for most pairs (0.01 for JPY pairs)

- Position Size = Contract size (100,000 for standard lot)

- Exchange Rate = Current rate (use 1.0000 if quote currency = account currency)

Cross Currency Position Sizing

When trading cross pairs (pairs not including your account currency), additional conversion is needed:

Example: Trading EUR/GBP with USD Account

Step 1: Calculate Base Position Size Position Size = Account Risk ÷ (Stop Distance × Base Pip Value)

Step 2: Convert Using GBP/USD Rate If GBP/USD = 1.2500: Adjusted Pip Value = Base Pip Value × 1.2500

Step 3: Recalculate Final Position Size Final Position Size = Account Risk ÷ (Stop Distance × Adjusted Pip Value)

The Percentage Distance Method

Alternative approach using percentage distance instead of pips:

Formula: Position Size = (Account Risk ÷ Percentage Distance) × (1 ÷ Entry Price) × Contract Size

When to Use:

- For precise percentage-based risk management

- When dealing with highly volatile pairs

- For automated trading system implementation

The Ultimate Stop-Loss

Position Sizing for Different Account Sizes

Small Accounts ($1,000 - $5,000)

Challenges:

- Limited position sizing flexibility

- Higher minimum risk percentages

- Micro lot requirements

Solutions:

- Use micro lots (1,000 units)

- Consider 2% risk for viable position sizes

- Focus on pairs with smaller pip values

Example Calculation:

- Account: $2,000

- Risk: 2% = $40

- Stop: 20 pips

- EUR/USD micro lot pip value: $0.10

- Position: $40 ÷ (20 × $0.10) = 20 micro lots

Medium Accounts ($5,000 - $50,000)

Advantages:

- Flexible position sizing with mini lots

- Standard 1% risk manageable

- Access to most currency pairs

Optimal Approach:

- 1% risk per trade

- Mix of mini and standard lots

- Full currency pair selection

Example Calculation:

- Account: $20,000

- Risk: 1% = $200

- Stop: 30 pips

- GBP/USD mini lot pip value: $1.00

- Position: $200 ÷ (30 × $1.00) = 200 mini lots = 2.0 standard lots

Large Accounts ($50,000+)

Advantages:

- Maximum flexibility

- Can use lower risk percentages

- Institutional-level position sizes

Professional Approach:

- 0.5-1% risk per trade

- Standard lot base calculations

- Advanced scaling strategies available

Example Calculation:

- Account: $100,000

- Risk: 0.5% = $500

- Stop: 40 pips

- USD/JPY standard lot pip value: $9.09

- Position: $500 ÷ (40 × $9.09) = 1.38 standard lots

The Ultimate Stop-Loss

Technology Solutions for Position Sizing

Excel/Google Sheets Calculators

Basic Formula Setup:

=B1/(B2*B3)

Where:

- B1 = Account Risk ($)

- B2 = Stop Distance (pips)

- B3 = Pip Value ($)

Advanced Calculator Features:

- Automatic pip value lookup tables

- Multiple currency pair support

- Risk percentage adjustment sliders

- Position size rounding functions

Trading Platform Calculators

MetaTrader Position Size Calculator:

- Built-in risk management tools

- Automatic pip value calculation

- Direct order placement integration

Professional Platform Features:

- Real-time pip value updates

- Multi-currency account support

- Advanced risk metrics display

Mobile Apps and Tools

The Ultimate Stop-Loss

Dedicated Position Sizing Apps:

- Forex Calculator Pro

- Position Size Calculator

- Risk Management Tools

Features to Look For:

- Offline calculation capability

- Currency pair databases

- Risk percentage presets

- Historical pip value data

Risk Scaling Formulas

The Kelly Criterion Adaptation

For advanced traders who want to scale risk based on win rate:

Kelly Formula: $f = (bp - q) \div b$

Where:

- f = Fraction of capital to risk

- b = Odds (average win ÷ average loss)

- p = Win probability

- q = Loss probability (1 - p)

Example Application:

- Win Rate: 60% (p = 0.6)

- Average Win: $150

- Average Loss: $100

- b = 150/100 = 1.5

The Ultimate Stop-Loss

- $f = (1.5 \times 0.6 - 0.4) \div 1.5 = 0.4 \div 1.5 = 0.267$

Suggests risking 26.7% per trade (typically scaled down to 1/4 of Kelly = 6.7%)

The Fixed Fractional Method

Formula: Position Size = (Account Balance × Risk Fraction) ÷ Stop Loss Amount

Benefits:

- Simple to implement

- Compounds gains automatically

- Reduces position sizes during drawdowns

Example:

- Account: $10,000

- Risk Fraction: 0.01 (1%)

- Stop Loss: $50

- Position Size: ($10,000 × 0.01) ÷ $50 = 2 units

Common Position Sizing Mistakes

Mistake #1: Ignoring Pip Value Differences

Wrong: Using same position size for EUR/USD and GBP/JPY **Right:** Calculate pip value for each pair separately

Mistake #2: Round Number Position Sizing

Wrong: Always trading 1.0 lots regardless of stop distance **Right:** Calculate exact position size for each trade setup

Mistake #3: Percentage Confusion

Wrong: Risking 1% of position size instead of account balance **Right:** Risk 1% of total account balance

Mistake #4: Not Adjusting for Account Growth

The Ultimate Stop-Loss

Wrong: Using fixed dollar amounts as account grows **Right:** Recalculate risk amounts as account balance changes

Mistake #5: Overcomplicating Calculations

Wrong: Using complex formulas that delay trade execution **Right:** Pre-calculate common scenarios for quick reference

Position Sizing Quick Reference Tables

EUR/USD Position Sizes (1% Risk)

Account Size	10 Pip Stop	20 Pip Stop	30 Pip Stop	40 Pip Stop
$5,000	5.0 lots	2.5 lots	1.67 lots	1.25 lots
$10,000	10.0 lots	5.0 lots	3.33 lots	2.5 lots
$25,000	25.0 lots	12.5 lots	8.33 lots	6.25 lots
$50,000	50.0 lots	25.0 lots	16.67 lots	12.5 lots

Note: Based on $1 per pip for mini lots

GBP/JPY Position Sizes (1% Risk, assuming $6.67 pip value)

Account Size	20 Pip Stop	40 Pip Stop	60 Pip Stop	80 Pip Stop
$5,000	3.75 lots	1.87 lots	1.25 lots	0.94 lots
$10,000	7.50 lots	3.75 lots	2.50 lots	1.87 lots
$25,000	18.75 lots	9.37 lots	6.25 lots	4.69 lots
$50,000	37.50 lots	18.75 lots	12.50 lots	9.37 lots

Practice Exercises

Exercise 1: Basic Position Sizing

Calculate position sizes for these scenarios:

1. Account: $15,000, Risk: 1%, EUR/USD, 25-pip stop

The Ultimate Stop-Loss

2. Account: $30,000, Risk: 0.5%, GBP/USD, 35-pip stop

3. Account: $8,000, Risk: 2%, USD/JPY, 45-pip stop

Exercise 2: Cross Currency Calculations

Calculate position sizes for non-USD account currencies:

1. EUR account trading GBP/JPY

2. GBP account trading EUR/USD

3. CAD account trading AUD/USD

Exercise 3: Scaling Scenarios

Calculate position sizes for 3-position scaling setup:

- Total risk: 1% of $20,000 account

- Position 1: 40% of total risk, 30-pip stop

- Position 2: 35% of total risk, 25-pip stop

- Position 3: 25% of total risk, 20-pip stop

Chapter 12 Summary: Position Sizing Mastery

Mathematical precision in position sizing transforms your trading:

1. **Universal Formula:** Position Size = Account Risk ÷ (Stop Distance × Pip Value)

2. **Consistent Risk:** Same percentage risk per trade regardless of stop distance

3. **Currency Awareness:** Different pairs require different pip value calculations

4. **Account Scaling:** Position sizes grow with account balance automatically

5. **Technology Integration:** Use calculators and tools for speed and accuracy

The Ultimate Stop-Loss

Perfect stop placement without proper position sizing is like having a perfect map but no compass. Master these calculations, and every trade becomes a precisely calculated risk with known potential outcomes.

Your position sizing should be so automatic that you never enter a trade without knowing exactly how much you're risking and why. This mathematical foundation supports everything else you've learned about stop loss mastery.

The Ultimate Stop-Loss

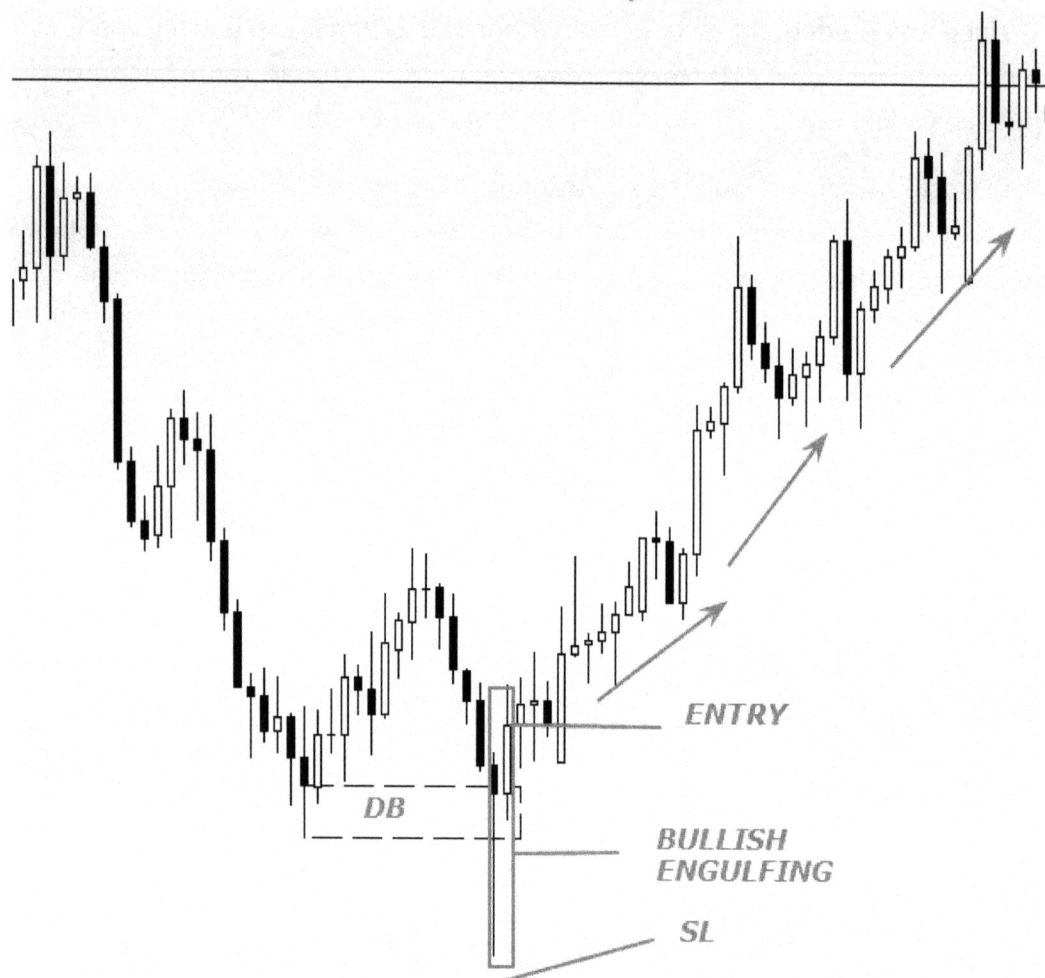

ENTRY

DB

BULLISH
ENGULFING

SL

Chapter 13: Risk Percentage Management

"A master trader doesn't risk the same amount in a hurricane as they do in calm seas. Risk percentage management is the art of adapting your exposure to market conditions while maintaining your edge."

Introduction: Beyond Fixed Risk

Most traders learn to risk 1% per trade and never evolve beyond this basic concept. While 1% is an excellent starting point, professional traders understand that optimal risk management requires flexibility based on market conditions, setup quality, and personal circumstances.

Chapter 13 will teach you when and how to adjust your risk percentages while maintaining strict discipline. You'll learn to increase risk when conditions are favorable and reduce it when caution is warranted, all while preserving your long-term profitability.

The core principle remains: never risk more than you can afford to lose. What changes is your ability to optimize risk based on probability, market conditions, and your trading performance.

The Dynamic Risk Framework

Base Risk Percentage: Your Foundation

Every trader needs a baseline risk percentage that represents their standard trade risk under normal conditions.

Conservative Approach: 0.5% per trade

- Suitable for new traders
- Preserves capital during learning phase
- Allows for many mistakes without account damage

Moderate Approach: 1% per trade

- Industry standard for most professionals

The Ultimate Stop-Loss

- Good balance between growth and preservation

- Suitable for experienced traders

Aggressive Approach: 2% per trade

- For highly experienced traders only

- Requires exceptional discipline

- Higher growth potential with increased risk

Risk Adjustment Factors

Professional traders adjust their base risk percentage based on five key factors:

1. **Setup Quality** (±0.5%)

2. **Market Conditions** (±0.3%)

3. **Personal Performance** (±0.2%)

4. **Account Drawdown Level** (±0.3%)

5. **Economic Calendar Impact** (±0.2%)

Maximum Risk Adjustment: ±1.5% from base (never exceed 3.5% total risk)

Setup Quality Risk Adjustment

High-Quality Setups (+0.3% to +0.5%)

Increase risk when multiple factors align in your favor:

Technical Confluence:

- Multiple timeframe alignment

- Key support/resistance test

- Perfect bullish/bearish engulfing pattern

- Volume confirmation

- Momentum divergence resolution

The Ultimate Stop-Loss

Example: EUR/USD Premium Setup

- Base Risk: 1%

- Setup Quality: +0.5% (multiple timeframe confluence)

- Final Risk: 1.5%

Rationale: When everything aligns perfectly, increase your bet size to maximize the opportunity.

Standard Setups (No Adjustment)

Maintain base risk for routine setups:

Normal Conditions:

- Single timeframe setup

- Standard bullish/bearish engulfing

- Moderate volume

- No special confluence factors

Example: GBP/USD Standard Setup

- Base Risk: 1%

- Setup Quality: No adjustment

- Final Risk: 1%

Low-Quality Setups (-0.3% to -0.5%)

Reduce risk when setup quality is questionable:

Warning Signs:

- Counter-trend trade without strong reason

- Poor volume confirmation

- Multiple recent false breakouts

- Unclear market structure

The Ultimate Stop-Loss

Example: USD/JPY Marginal Setup

- Base Risk: 1%

- Setup Quality: -0.3% (counter-trend in strong market)

- Final Risk: 0.7%

Decision Point: Consider not taking low-quality setups at all.

Market Conditions Risk Adjustment

High Volatility Periods (-0.2% to -0.3%)

Reduce risk during exceptionally volatile markets:

High Volatility Indicators:

- VIX above 25

- Major news events pending

- Geopolitical uncertainty

- Market gaps and unusual price action

Adjustment Rationale:

- Stops more likely to be hit by noise

- Increased slippage risk

- Emotional stress higher

- False signals more common

Example: During Brexit Referendum

- Base Risk: 1%

- Market Conditions: -0.3% (extreme uncertainty)

- Final Risk: 0.7%

Normal Volatility (No Adjustment)

The Ultimate Stop-Loss

Maintain standard risk during typical market conditions:

Normal Market Characteristics:

- VIX between 12-25

- Regular news flow

- Predictable session patterns

- Standard price movements

Low Volatility Periods (+0.1% to +0.2%)

Slightly increase risk during stable conditions:

Low Volatility Indicators:

- VIX below 12

- Summer holiday periods

- Established trending markets

- Clear support/resistance levels

Caution: Don't dramatically increase risk as low volatility can end suddenly.

Example: August Trading

- Base Risk: 1%

- Market Conditions: +0.1% (summer doldrums)

- Final Risk: 1.1%

Personal Performance Risk Adjustment

Hot Streak Management (+0.1% to +0.2%)

Slightly increase risk during winning streaks:

Hot Streak Criteria:

- 5+ consecutive winners

The Ultimate Stop-Loss

- Above-average profit per trade

- Clear decision-making confidence

- No revenge trading tendencies

Conservative Increase:

- Maximum +0.2% adjustment

- Monitor for overconfidence

- Ready to reduce quickly if streak ends

Example: After 6 Consecutive Winners

- Base Risk: 1%

- Performance Adjustment: +0.2%

- Final Risk: 1.2%

Cold Streak Management (-0.2% to -0.5%)

Reduce risk during losing periods:

Cold Streak Indicators:

- 4+ consecutive losses

- Below-average win rate

- Emotional decision making

- Questioning your system

Protective Reduction:

- Immediate risk reduction

- Focus on process over profits

- Consider trading break if severe

Example: After 5 Consecutive Losses

- Base Risk: 1%

- Performance Adjustment: -0.3%

- Final Risk: 0.7%

Normal Performance (No Adjustment)

Maintain base risk during typical performance periods:

Balanced Performance:

- Mix of winners and losers

- Consistent with historical results

- Emotionally stable trading

- System confidence intact

Account Drawdown Risk Adjustment

Maximum Drawdown Protection

Implement systematic risk reduction as drawdown increases:

Drawdown Levels and Risk Adjustments:

- 0-5% drawdown: No adjustment

- 5-10% drawdown: -0.1% risk reduction

- 10-15% drawdown: -0.2% risk reduction

- 15-20% drawdown: -0.3% risk reduction

- 20%+ drawdown: Stop trading, review system

Example: Account at 12% Drawdown

- Base Risk: 1%

- Drawdown Adjustment: -0.2%

- Final Risk: 0.8%

The Ultimate Stop-Loss

Recovery Phase Management

As account recovers, gradually return to normal risk:

Recovery Protocol:

- Wait for drawdown to improve by 5% before increasing risk

- Increase risk in 0.1% increments

- Monitor for sustainable recovery

- Full risk restoration only after returning to previous highs

Example: Drawdown Improving from 15% to 8%

- Previous Risk: 0.7% (during 15% drawdown)

- Current Risk: 0.9% (gradual increase)

- Target Risk: 1% (when drawdown under 5%)

Economic Calendar Risk Adjustment

High-Impact News Periods (-0.1% to -0.2%)

Reduce risk around major economic announcements:

High-Impact Events:

- Central bank decisions

- Employment reports (NFP)

- Inflation data (CPI)

- GDP releases

Pre-News Strategy:

- Reduce new position risk 2 hours before

- Consider closing short-term positions

- Prepare for increased volatility

The Ultimate Stop-Loss

Example: Day of Federal Reserve Decision

- Base Risk: 1%

- News Impact: -0.2%

- Final Risk: 0.8%

News-Heavy Weeks (-0.1%)

Slight risk reduction during weeks with multiple high-impact events:

Multiple Event Weeks:

- Central bank week

- Employment data + inflation

- Multiple GDP releases

- Election periods

Example: Central Bank Week (Fed, ECB, BOJ)

- Base Risk: 1%

- Multiple Events: -0.1%

- Final Risk: 0.9%

Advanced Risk Management Concepts

The Risk Budget System

Allocate your total weekly/monthly risk across different opportunity levels:

Weekly Risk Budget: 5% of Account

- High-Quality Setups: 3% allocation

- Standard Setups: 1.5% allocation

- Opportunistic Trades: 0.5% allocation

Benefits:

The Ultimate Stop-Loss

- Prevents overtrading

- Ensures capital for best opportunities

- Natural position sizing discipline

Correlation-Adjusted Risk

Reduce individual trade risk when holding correlated positions:

High Correlation Pairs:

- EUR/USD and GBP/USD

- AUD/USD and NZD/USD

- USD/JPY and USD/CHF

Adjustment Method: If holding EUR/USD, reduce GBP/USD risk by 0.2-0.3%

Example:

- Current Position: 1% risk on EUR/USD long

- New Opportunity: GBP/USD long setup

- Adjusted Risk: 0.7% (reduced for correlation)

Time-Decay Risk Management

Adjust risk based on how long you plan to hold positions:

Scalping Trades (Minutes to Hours):

- Slightly higher risk acceptable (up to +0.2%)

- Quick exits limit exposure time

- Less overnight risk

Swing Trades (Days to Weeks):

- Standard risk levels

- Account for weekend gaps

The Ultimate Stop-Loss

- Consider position holding costs

Long-Term Positions (Weeks to Months):

- Slightly reduced risk (-0.1% to -0.2%)

- Account for fundamental changes

- Higher uncertainty over time

Risk Percentage Calculation Examples

Example 1: Premium EUR/USD Setup

Base Setup:

- Account: $25,000

- Base Risk: 1%

- Entry: 1.0950

- Stop: 1.0920 (30 pips)

Risk Adjustments:

- Setup Quality: +0.4% (triple timeframe confluence)

- Market Conditions: 0% (normal volatility)

- Performance: +0.1% (recent winner)

- Drawdown: 0% (account at highs)

- News: -0.1% (ECB tomorrow)

Final Calculation:

- Final Risk: 1% + 0.4% + 0% + 0.1% + 0% - 0.1% = 1.4%

- Risk Amount: $25,000 × 1.4% = $350

- Position Size: $350 ÷ (30 pips × $1) = 35 mini lots = 3.5 standard lots

Example 2: Marginal GBP/JPY Setup

The Ultimate Stop-Loss

Base Setup:

- Account: $50,000

- Base Risk: 1%

- Entry: 185.20

- Stop: 184.70 (50 pips)

Risk Adjustments:

- Setup Quality: -0.3% (counter-trend)

- Market Conditions: -0.2% (high volatility)

- Performance: -0.2% (recent losses)

- Drawdown: -0.1% (8% drawdown)

- News: 0% (no major events)

Final Calculation:

- Final Risk: 1% - 0.3% - 0.2% - 0.2% - 0.1% + 0% = 0.2%

- Risk Amount: $50,000 × 0.2% = $100

- Position Size: $100 ÷ (50 pips × $6.67) = 0.3 standard lots

Decision: Consider skipping this trade due to very low adjusted risk.

Technology Integration

Risk Management Spreadsheets

Daily Risk Calculator:

- Account balance input

- Base risk percentage

- Adjustment factor inputs

- Automatic final risk calculation

- Position size output

Weekly Risk Budget Tracker:

- Total weekly risk allocation

- Used vs. remaining budget

- Quality-based allocation tracking

Trading Platform Integration

Custom Indicators:

- Account drawdown display

- Risk percentage calculator

- Position correlation warnings

- News event alerts

Automated Risk Adjustment:

- Based on account balance changes

- Drawdown protection triggers

- Performance-based modifications

Risk Percentage Mistakes to Avoid

Mistake #1: Dramatic Risk Increases

Wrong: Doubling risk after a big winner **Right:** Maximum +0.5% adjustment from base

Mistake #2: Ignoring Drawdown Signals

Wrong: Maintaining full risk during 20% drawdown **Right:** Systematic risk reduction as drawdowns increase

Mistake #3: News Event Overconfidence

The Ultimate Stop-Loss

Wrong: Increasing risk before major announcements **Right:** Reducing risk due to uncertainty

Mistake #4: Correlation Blindness

Wrong: Full risk on EUR/USD and GBP/USD simultaneously **Right:** Adjusted risk for correlated positions

Mistake #5: Emotional Risk Adjustments

Wrong: Changing risk based on fear or greed **Right:** Systematic adjustments based on objective criteria

Risk Management Rules Summary

The Golden Rules of Dynamic Risk

1. **Never exceed 3.5% total risk** regardless of adjustments

2. **Base risk should represent 70%+ of your trades**

3. **Document all risk adjustment decisions**

4. **Review and adjust criteria monthly**

5. **Reduce risk immediately when in doubt**

The Risk Reduction Hierarchy

When multiple negative factors align, use this priority system:

1. **Account protection** (drawdown) - highest priority

2. **Performance protection** (cold streaks) - high priority

3. **Market protection** (volatility) - medium priority

4. **Setup quality** (poor setups) - medium priority

5. **News protection** (events) - lower priority

Chapter 13 Summary: Dynamic Risk Mastery

Risk percentage management elevates your trading from mechanical to adaptive:

The Ultimate Stop-Loss

1. **Base Foundation:** Establish your standard risk percentage (0.5-2%)

2. **Systematic Adjustments:** Use objective criteria to modify risk

3. **Maximum Limits:** Never exceed 3.5% total risk on any single trade

4. **Drawdown Protection:** Reduce risk systematically as losses mount

5. **Quality Recognition:** Increase risk for exceptional opportunities

6. **Market Adaptation:** Adjust for volatility and news events

Dynamic risk management allows you to optimize your edge while protecting your capital. The best traders are not those who risk the same amount on every trade, but those who risk the right amount based on current conditions.

Master this skill, and you'll find yourself naturally positioned for maximum gains during favorable periods while minimizing damage during challenging times. Your risk management becomes as dynamic and responsive as the markets themselves.

The Ultimate Stop-Loss

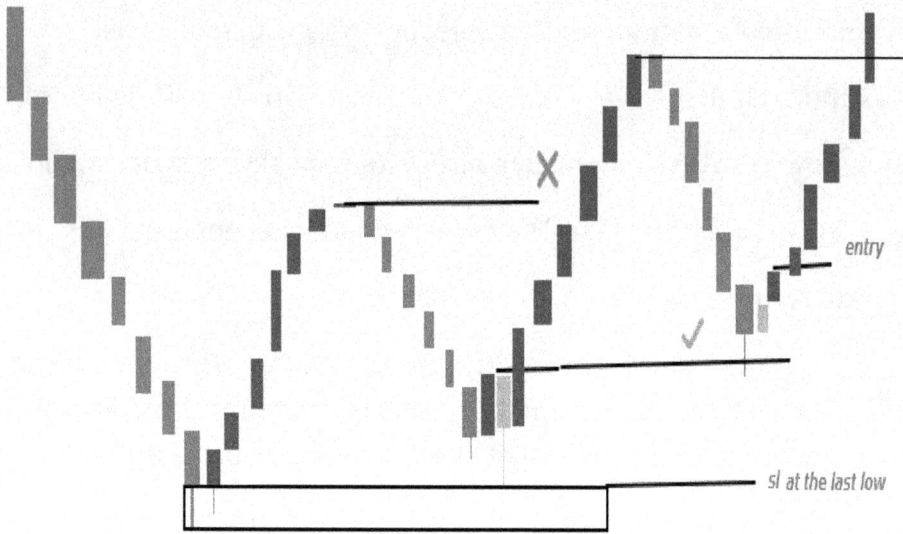

entry

X

✓

sl at the last low

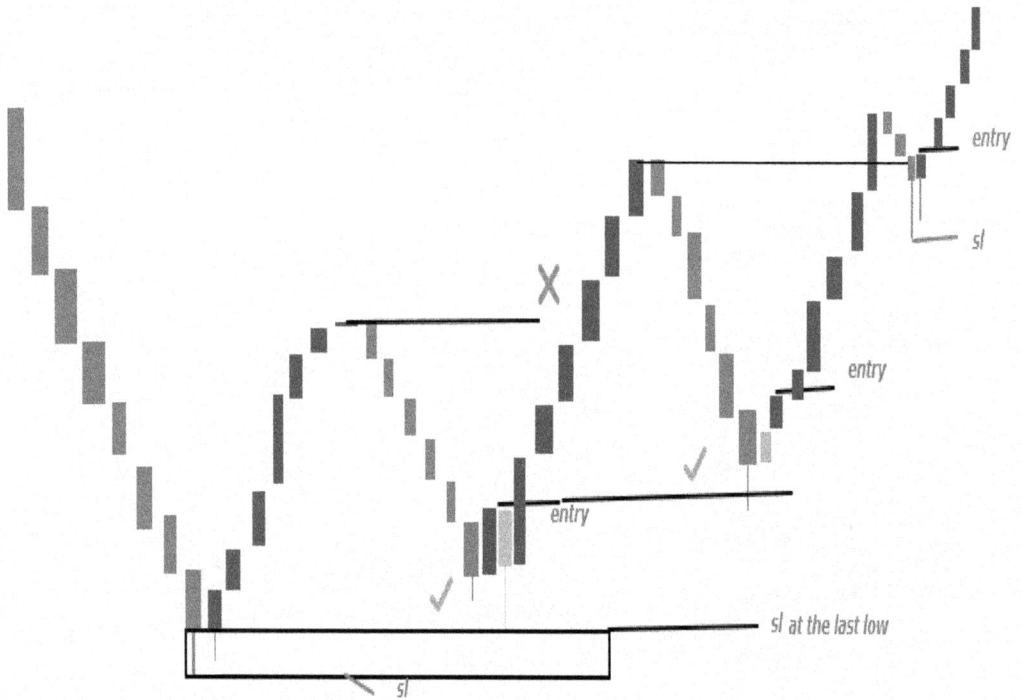

entry

sl

X

entry

✓

entry

✓

sl at the last low

sl

Chapter 14: Account Growth Projections

"A trader without growth projections is like a captain without a destination. You might sail skillfully, but you'll never know if you're heading toward prosperity or drifting toward mediocrity."

Introduction: The Mathematics of Wealth Building

You've mastered stop loss placement, position sizing, and dynamic risk management. Now it's time to understand how these skills compound into long-term wealth creation. Chapter 14 will show you how to project account growth realistically, set achievable goals, and track your progress toward financial independence.

Understanding growth projections serves three critical purposes: it sets realistic expectations, helps you make informed decisions about risk levels, and provides motivation during inevitable drawdown periods.

The key insight is that consistent profitability, even at modest monthly returns, creates extraordinary wealth over time through the power of compounding. Small edges, properly managed, become life-changing advantages.

The Foundation of Growth Projections

The Compound Growth Formula

Account growth follows the mathematical principle of compound interest:

Future Value = Present Value × (1 + Monthly Return)^Number of Months

Example:

- Starting Account: $10,000

- Monthly Return: 3%

- Time Period: 24 months

- Future Value: $10,000 × (1.03)^24 = $20,328

This simple formula reveals the extraordinary power of consistency over time.

The Ultimate Stop-Loss

Key Variables in Growth Projections

Monthly Return Rate:

- Conservative: 2-4% per month

- Moderate: 5-8% per month

- Aggressive: 10%+ per month

Win Rate:

- Your percentage of winning trades

- Typically 45-65% for trend followers

- Higher win rates often mean smaller average wins

Risk-to-Reward Ratio:

- Average win divided by average loss

- Professional targets: 1.5:1 to 3:1

- Higher ratios compensate for lower win rates

Monthly Trading Frequency:

- Number of trades per month

- Affects compounding frequency

- More trades ≠ better results

Realistic Growth Scenarios

Conservative Growth Model (2-4% Monthly)

Characteristics:

- 0.5-1% risk per trade

- High-quality setups only

- Focus on capital preservation

The Ultimate Stop-Loss

- Suitable for retirement accounts

10-Year Projection Starting with $25,000:

- 2% monthly: $25,000 → $202,000

- 3% monthly: $25,000 → $486,000

- 4% monthly: $25,000 → $1,158,000

Trade Requirements for 3% Monthly:

- Win Rate: 60%

- Risk-Reward: 2:1

- Trades per Month: 8

- Risk per Trade: 1%

Moderate Growth Model (5-8% Monthly)

Characteristics:

- 1-2% risk per trade

- Good setup selection

- Balanced growth/preservation

- Suitable for active traders

10-Year Projection Starting with $50,000:

- 5% monthly: $50,000 → $814,000

- 6% monthly: $50,000 → $1,284,000

- 7% monthly: $50,000 → $2,017,000

- 8% monthly: $50,000 → $3,162,000

Trade Requirements for 6% Monthly:

- Win Rate: 55%

The Ultimate Stop-Loss

- Risk-Reward: 2.5:1

- Trades per Month: 12

- Risk per Trade: 1.5%

Aggressive Growth Model (10%+ Monthly)

Characteristics:

- 2-3% risk per trade

- Higher frequency trading

- Maximum growth focus

- Requires exceptional skill

10-Year Projection Starting with $100,000:

- 10% monthly: $100,000 → $3,138,000

- 12% monthly: $100,000 → $5,744,000

- 15% monthly: $100,000 → $13,181,000

Trade Requirements for 10% Monthly:

- Win Rate: 50%

- Risk-Reward: 3:1

- Trades per Month: 15

- Risk per Trade: 2%

Warning: These returns require exceptional skill and carry significant risk of substantial drawdowns.

The Reality of Drawdowns

Understanding Drawdown Impact

Even profitable systems experience periods of losses. Understanding drawdown recovery is crucial for realistic projections.

The Ultimate Stop-Loss

Drawdown Recovery Table:

- 10% drawdown requires 11.1% gain to recover

- 20% drawdown requires 25% gain to recover

- 30% drawdown requires 42.9% gain to recover

- 50% drawdown requires 100% gain to recover

Example: $100,000 Account with 20% Drawdown

- Account drops to $80,000

- Needs $20,000 gain (25% of $80,000) to recover

- At 5% monthly, recovery takes 5.6 months

Maximum Drawdown Expectations

Conservative Systems: 15-25% maximum drawdown **Moderate Systems:** 25-35% maximum drawdown **Aggressive Systems:** 35-50% maximum drawdown

Planning for Drawdowns:

- Expect maximum drawdowns to occur

- Plan risk reduction strategies

- Maintain 6-12 months living expenses separate

- Don't panic during normal drawdown periods

Account Size Milestones and Strategies

Small Account Phase ($1,000 - $10,000)

Primary Goals:

- Skill development over profit maximization

- Prove system profitability

- Build trading confidence

The Ultimate Stop-Loss

- Establish consistent habits

Growth Strategy:

- 2-5% monthly targets
- Focus on process over profits
- No withdrawals during growth phase
- Micro and mini lot trading

Milestone Targets:

- $1,000 → $5,000 (quintuple account)
- $5,000 → $10,000 (double account)
- Timeline: 18-36 months

Medium Account Phase ($10,000 - $100,000)

Primary Goals:

- Consistent profitability demonstration
- Risk management refinement
- System optimization
- Professional development

Growth Strategy:

- 3-7% monthly targets
- Begin selective withdrawals (20% of profits)
- Standard lot capability
- Advanced strategies implementation

Milestone Targets:

- $10,000 → $25,000 (2.5x growth)

The Ultimate Stop-Loss

- $25,000 → $50,000 (2x growth)

- $50,000 → $100,000 (2x growth)

- Timeline: 3-5 years

Large Account Phase ($100,000+)

Primary Goals:

- Wealth preservation with growth

- Income generation capability

- Professional money management

- Financial independence preparation

Growth Strategy:

- 2-5% monthly targets (more conservative)

- Regular withdrawals (30-50% of profits)

- Institutional-level risk management

- Multiple strategy diversification

Income Generation:

- $100,000 at 4% monthly = $4,000/month income

- $500,000 at 3% monthly = $15,000/month income

- $1,000,000 at 2% monthly = $20,000/month income

Setting Realistic Goals and Timelines

The 5-Year Wealth Building Plan

Year 1: Foundation Building

- Starting Capital: $10,000

- Target Monthly Return: 3%

The Ultimate Stop-Loss

- End of Year 1: $14,257

- Focus: Skill development, consistency

Year 2: System Optimization

- Starting Capital: $14,257

- Target Monthly Return: 4%

- End of Year 2: $22,879

- Focus: Risk management, scaling

Year 3: Growth Acceleration

- Starting Capital: $22,879

- Target Monthly Return: 5%

- End of Year 3: $41,137

- Focus: Advanced strategies, confidence

Year 4: Wealth Building

- Starting Capital: $41,137

- Target Monthly Return: 5%

- End of Year 4: $73,947

- Focus: Consistency, larger positions

Year 5: Approaching Independence

- Starting Capital: $73,947

- Target Monthly Return: 4%

- End of Year 5: $118,077

- Focus: Preservation, income generation

5-Year Result: $10,000 → $118,077 (11.8x growth)

The Ultimate Stop-Loss

Monthly Income Milestones

Financial Independence Levels:

Basic Living ($3,000/month):

- Need: $150,000 at 2% monthly

- Or: $100,000 at 3% monthly

- Or: $75,000 at 4% monthly

Comfortable Living ($6,000/month):

- Need: $300,000 at 2% monthly

- Or: $200,000 at 3% monthly

- Or: $150,000 at 4% monthly

Luxury Living ($15,000/month):

- Need: $750,000 at 2% monthly

- Or: $500,000 at 3% monthly

- Or: $375,000 at 4% monthly

Growth Tracking and Measurement

Key Performance Metrics

Monthly Return Rate:

- Track actual vs. projected returns

- Identify trends and patterns

- Adjust projections based on performance

Sharpe Ratio:

- Measures return per unit of risk

- Formula: (Return - Risk-Free Rate) ÷ Standard Deviation

The Ultimate Stop-Loss

- Higher ratios indicate better risk-adjusted returns

Maximum Drawdown:

- Track largest peak-to-trough decline
- Compare to system expectations
- Trigger risk reduction if exceeded

Win Rate and Risk-Reward:

- Monitor changes over time
- Ensure they align with projections
- Adjust expectations as needed

Monthly Review Process

Performance Analysis:

1. Calculate actual monthly return
2. Compare to projected return
3. Analyze significant deviations
4. Identify improvement areas

Projection Updates:

1. Update growth projections based on actual performance
2. Adjust risk levels if needed
3. Revise timeline estimates
4. Set next month's targets

Documentation:

- Maintain detailed growth records
- Track milestone achievements

The Ultimate Stop-Loss

- Document strategy changes

- Review goal progress

The Psychology of Growth

Managing Expectations

Realistic Expectations:

- Growth is not linear

- Drawdown periods are normal

- Consistency beats perfection

- Time is your greatest ally

Unrealistic Expectations:

- Doubling account monthly

- No losing months

- Guaranteed returns

- Get-rich-quick outcomes

Compound Growth Mindset

The Power of Patience:

- Small consistent gains compound dramatically

- Year 1-3 feel slow, Year 4-10 accelerate

- Focus on process, not immediate results

- Celebrate small milestones

Avoiding Growth Killers:

- Overtrading after good months

- Increasing risk dramatically

The Ultimate Stop-Loss

- Withdrawing too much too early

- Abandoning system during drawdowns

Advanced Growth Strategies

Multiple Account Strategy

Strategy Benefits:

- Risk diversification

- Different growth rates

- Tax optimization

- Psychological benefits

Account Allocation Example:

- Conservative Account (60%): 2-3% monthly target

- Moderate Account (30%): 4-6% monthly target

- Aggressive Account (10%): 8-12% monthly target

Scaling Risk with Account Size

Dynamic Risk Adjustment:

- Small accounts: Higher risk (2-3%)

- Medium accounts: Moderate risk (1-2%)

- Large accounts: Conservative risk (0.5-1%)

Rationale:

- Small accounts need growth

- Large accounts need preservation

- Risk tolerance changes with wealth

Withdrawal Strategies

The Ultimate Stop-Loss

No Withdrawal Phase (Months 1-12):

- Maximize compounding

- Build substantial base

- Prove system viability

Partial Withdrawal Phase (Year 2-5):

- Withdraw 20-30% of monthly profits

- Enjoy some benefits of trading

- Continue strong growth

Income Generation Phase (Year 5+):

- Withdraw 50-70% of monthly profits

- Focus on consistent income

- Preserve capital base

Real-World Growth Examples

Case Study 1: Conservative Trader "Sarah"

Starting Conditions:

- Initial Capital: $15,000

- Risk per Trade: 1%

- Target Monthly Return: 3%

- Strategy: High-quality setups only

Year 1 Results:

- Actual Monthly Return: 2.8%

- Ending Balance: $20,547

- Maximum Drawdown: 12%

- Trade Frequency: 6 trades/month

Year 3 Results:

- Account Value: $36,918

- Monthly Income Potential: $1,100

- Confidence Level: High

- Ready to increase targets

Case Study 2: Moderate Trader "Marcus"

Starting Conditions:

- Initial Capital: $25,000

- Risk per Trade: 1.5%

- Target Monthly Return: 5%

- Strategy: Balanced approach

Year 1 Results:

- Actual Monthly Return: 4.2%

- Ending Balance: $38,945

- Maximum Drawdown: 18%

- Trade Frequency: 10 trades/month

Year 5 Results:

- Account Value: $186,234

- Monthly Income Potential: $7,450

- Status: Approaching independence

- Strategy: Becoming more conservative

Case Study 3: Aggressive Trader "David"

The Ultimate Stop-Loss

Starting Conditions:

- Initial Capital: $50,000
- Risk per Trade: 2.5%
- Target Monthly Return: 8%
- Strategy: High-frequency trading

Year 1 Results:

- Actual Monthly Return: 6.8%
- Ending Balance: $106,543
- Maximum Drawdown: 28%
- Trade Frequency: 15 trades/month

Challenges Faced:

- Large drawdown in Month 8
- Emotional stress during losses
- Required risk reduction
- Learned discipline importance

Technology for Growth Tracking

Spreadsheet Solutions

Growth Projection Calculator:

- Input starting capital and monthly return
- Automatic future value calculations
- Scenario comparison features
- Chart generation capability

Performance Tracker:

- Monthly return tracking

- Drawdown monitoring

- Goal progress measurement

- Milestone celebration alerts

Professional Software

Trading Journal Programs:

- Automated performance analysis

- Risk-adjusted return calculations

- Drawdown statistics

- Growth projection updates

Portfolio Management Tools:

- Multi-account tracking

- Risk allocation monitoring

- Performance attribution analysis

- Tax reporting preparation

Mobile Apps

Account Monitoring:

- Real-time balance tracking

- Performance notifications

- Goal progress updates

- Motivational milestone alerts

Chapter 14 Summary: Growth Mastery Keys

Account growth projections transform trading from gambling to wealth building:

The Ultimate Stop-Loss

1. **Compound Power:** Small consistent returns create extraordinary long-term wealth

2. **Realistic Expectations:** 2-8% monthly returns are achievable and life-changing

3. **Drawdown Planning:** Expect and prepare for temporary setbacks

4. **Milestone Thinking:** Break long-term goals into achievable steps

5. **Performance Tracking:** Monitor progress and adjust projections accordingly

6. **Growth Strategy Evolution:** Adjust risk and withdrawal rates as account grows

The mathematics of wealth building reveal that you don't need to hit home runs to achieve financial independence. Singles and doubles, consistently executed over time, build more wealth than attempting dramatic gains.

Your stop loss mastery, combined with proper position sizing and dynamic risk management, creates the foundation for predictable account growth. The projections in this chapter aren't fantasies—they're achievable outcomes for disciplined traders who master the fundamentals.

Remember: the goal isn't to get rich quickly, but to get rich surely. Time and consistency are your greatest allies in the wealth-building journey.

Chapter 15: Daily Affirmations and Mental Exercises

"The battlefield of trading is won or lost in the mind before the first position is ever opened. Master your psychology, and the profits will follow."

Introduction: The Mental Game of Trading

You've mastered the technical aspects of stop loss placement, position sizing, and risk management. But trading success ultimately depends on your ability to execute these skills consistently under pressure. Chapter 15 addresses the psychological foundation that separates profitable traders from the majority who struggle.

The most sophisticated trading system in the world becomes worthless if you can't execute it with discipline and emotional control. This chapter provides practical tools to strengthen your trading psychology through daily mental exercises and reinforcing affirmations.

Professional traders understand that mindset work isn't optional—it's the foundation upon which all technical skills rest. The exercises in this chapter will help you develop the mental resilience needed for long-term trading success.

The Psychology of Stop Loss Mastery

Mental Barriers to Proper Stop Placement

Fear-Based Barriers:

- Fear of small losses leading to tight stops
- Fear of being wrong causing hesitation
- Fear of missing out driving poor timing
- Fear of large stops preventing proper placement

Ego-Based Barriers:

The Ultimate Stop-Loss

- Refusing to admit when wrong

- Moving stops to avoid losses

- Overconfidence after wins

- Underestimating market randomness

Greed-Based Barriers:

- Risking too much for potential profits

- Ignoring stop rules for "sure thing" trades

- Scaling position sizes too aggressively

- Holding losing trades hoping for recovery

The Disciplined Trader's Mindset

Core Beliefs of Successful Traders:

1. Losses are part of the business, not personal failures

2. Stop losses protect capital for future opportunities

3. Consistent execution beats perfect market timing

4. Risk management creates long-term wealth

5. Discipline under pressure separates professionals from amateurs

Daily Affirmation System

Morning Trading Affirmations

Begin each trading day by reading these affirmations aloud with conviction:

Risk Management Affirmations:

"I risk only what I can afford to lose on every trade."

- Reinforces proper position sizing discipline

- Prevents emotional attachment to outcomes

The Ultimate Stop-Loss

- Maintains long-term perspective

"My stop loss is my best friend and protector of capital."

- Reframes stops as positive tools

- Reduces emotional resistance to taking losses

- Builds confidence in risk management system

"I place my stops at the last low when buying and last high when selling."

- Reinforces core technical rules

- Prevents second-guessing placement decisions

- Builds automatic response patterns

"I execute my trading plan with precision and discipline."

- Emphasizes systematic approach

- Reduces impulsive decision making

- Builds confidence in preparation

"Every loss brings me closer to my next winning trade."

- Reframes losses as progress toward goals

- Maintains positive outlook during difficult periods

- Encourages persistence through drawdowns

Confidence Building Affirmations:

"I am a skilled trader who makes informed decisions based on proven principles."

- Builds self-confidence in abilities

- Reinforces systematic approach

- Counters imposter syndrome

"I trust my analysis and execute trades with conviction."

The Ultimate Stop-Loss

- Reduces second-guessing and hesitation

- Builds decisive action habits

- Strengthens commitment to system

"I learn from every trade, whether it wins or loses."

- Maintains growth mindset

- Reduces perfectionism pressure

- Encourages continuous improvement

"I am patient and wait for high-quality setups that meet my criteria."

- Prevents overtrading

- Reinforces quality over quantity approach

- Builds discipline during slow periods

"I am building long-term wealth through consistent, disciplined trading."

- Maintains long-term perspective

- Counters get-rich-quick mentality

- Builds patience for compound growth

Evening Reflection Affirmations

End each trading day with these reflective affirmations:

Performance Review Affirmations:

"I followed my trading rules today and am proud of my discipline."

- Reinforces positive behaviors

- Builds consistency habits

- Creates sense of accomplishment

"I learned valuable lessons from today's trades that will improve my future performance."

The Ultimate Stop-Loss

- Maintains learning mindset

- Reduces regret over mistakes

- Encourages continuous development

"I am grateful for the opportunity to build wealth through trading."

- Maintains positive attitude

- Reduces stress and anxiety

- Builds appreciation for opportunities

"Tomorrow I will trade with even greater precision and confidence."

- Sets positive expectations

- Programs subconscious for improvement

- Builds momentum for next session

Mental Exercises for Trading Excellence

Exercise 1: Visualization Techniques

Perfect Trade Execution Visualization (10 minutes daily):

1. **Setup Phase:**

   o Sit comfortably with eyes closed

   o Take 5 deep breaths to center yourself

   o Visualize your trading workspace clearly

2. **Trade Identification:**

   o See yourself analyzing charts methodically

   o Visualize identifying a perfect setup

   o See the bullish/bearish engulfing pattern clearly

   o Feel confident in your analysis

3. **Stop Placement:**

    o   Visualize placing stop at the last low/high

    o   See yourself calculating position size precisely

    o   Feel calm and systematic in your approach

    o   Experience confidence in your risk management

4. **Trade Execution:**

    o   Visualize entering the trade at the right moment

    o   See the trade moving in your favor

    o   Experience the satisfaction of proper execution

    o   Feel proud of following your system

5. **Outcome Acceptance:**

    o   Visualize both winning and losing scenarios

    o   See yourself accepting either outcome calmly

    o   Feel grateful for proper risk management

    o   Experience confidence in long-term approach

Benefits:

- Programs subconscious for correct behaviors

- Reduces anxiety about trade execution

- Builds confidence through mental rehearsal

- Improves actual performance under pressure

Exercise 2: Stress Inoculation Training

Drawdown Resilience Exercise (15 minutes, 2x per week):

1. **Scenario Setup:**

The Ultimate Stop-Loss

- Imagine your account in a 15% drawdown

- Visualize recent losing trades

- Feel the natural emotions arising

- Don't resist the uncomfortable feelings

2. **Response Training:**

   - Practice your systematic response

   - Visualize reducing position sizes appropriately

   - See yourself reviewing and following your rules

   - Experience calm decision-making under pressure

3. **Perspective Shift:**

   - Remember that drawdowns are temporary

   - Visualize past recoveries from similar situations

   - Feel confidence in your proven system

   - Experience determination to continue

4. **Action Planning:**

   - Visualize taking constructive actions

   - See yourself analyzing trades objectively

   - Feel motivated to improve and continue

   - Experience pride in professional response

Benefits:

- Builds resilience for real drawdown periods

- Reduces emotional impact of losses

- Practices professional responses to stress

- Builds confidence in system recovery

Exercise 3: Discipline Reinforcement Training

Temptation Resistance Exercise (10 minutes daily):

1. **Common Temptation Scenarios:**

   - Visualize wanting to move a stop loss

   - See yourself tempted to overtrade

   - Feel the urge to risk more than planned

   - Experience FOMO on a setup

2. **Response Practice:**

   - Visualize stopping and taking a breath

   - See yourself remembering your rules

   - Feel the strength to resist temptation

   - Experience pride in maintaining discipline

3. **Consequence Visualization:**

   - See the positive results of discipline

   - Visualize long-term account growth

   - Feel pride in professional behavior

   - Experience confidence in your system

Benefits:

- Strengthens discipline under pressure

- Builds automatic resistance to poor decisions

- Reinforces long-term thinking

- Reduces impulsive trading behaviors

The Ultimate Stop-Loss

Exercise 4: Confidence Building Meditation

Trading Confidence Meditation (15 minutes, daily):

1. **Relaxation Phase (5 minutes):**

   o   Find comfortable seated position

   o   Focus on slow, deep breathing

   o   Release physical tension

   o   Quiet mental chatter

2. **Competence Affirmation (5 minutes):**

   o   Repeat: "I am a skilled and disciplined trader"

   o   Feel the truth of this statement

   o   Remember past successful trades

   o   Experience growing confidence

3. **System Trust Building (5 minutes):**

   o   Visualize your trading system working

   o   See consistent profitability over time

   o   Feel trust in your proven methods

   o   Experience calm confidence in approach

Benefits:

- Builds unshakeable self-confidence

- Reduces anxiety and fear

- Strengthens trust in systematic approach

- Improves overall trading performance

Psychological Exercises for Specific Challenges

The Ultimate Stop-Loss

Overcoming Fear of Losses

Loss Acceptance Exercise:

1. **Acknowledge the Fear:**
   - Admit that you fear losing money
   - Recognize this as normal and human
   - Don't judge yourself for having fear
   - Accept fear as part of trading

2. **Reframe Losses:**
   - View losses as business expenses
   - See stops as insurance premiums
   - Consider losses as learning investments
   - Frame losses as progress toward profits

3. **Quantify Risk:**
   - Calculate exactly what you're risking
   - Ensure it's money you can afford to lose
   - Feel comfortable with the risk amount
   - Experience peace with potential loss

4. **Focus on Process:**
   - Concentrate on following your system
   - Measure success by rule adherence
   - Take pride in disciplined execution
   - Let profits be byproduct of good process

Managing Winning Streaks

The Ultimate Stop-Loss

Success Humility Exercise:

1. **Acknowledge Success:**

   o Celebrate your winning trades

   o Feel proud of disciplined execution

   o Recognize your skill development

   o Appreciate your hard work paying off

2. **Maintain Perspective:**

   o Remember that markets are unpredictable

   o Acknowledge role of luck in short-term results

   o Stay focused on long-term consistency

   o Avoid overconfidence trap

3. **Reinforce Discipline:**

   o Commit to following rules during wins

   o Resist urge to increase risk dramatically

   o Stay systematic in approach

   o Plan for inevitable losing periods

Handling Losing Streaks

Resilience Building Exercise:

1. **Accept Reality:**

   o Acknowledge that losing streaks happen

   o Recognize them as normal part of trading

   o Don't take losses personally

   o Maintain professional perspective

2. **Review System:**

   - Analyze if system is being followed correctly

   - Check for any rule violations

   - Confirm system logic remains sound

   - Make adjustments only if objectively needed

3. **Reduce Risk:**

   - Lower position sizes during drawdowns

   - Focus on capital preservation

   - Maintain discipline despite frustration

   - Trust in system recovery

4. **Maintain Hope:**

   - Remember past recoveries

   - Focus on long-term track record

   - Visualize future success

   - Stay committed to proven approach

Daily Mental Routine Structure

Pre-Market Routine (20 minutes)

Minutes 1-5: Centering

- Deep breathing exercises

- Physical tension release

- Mental clarity preparation

- Emotional state assessment

Minutes 6-10: Affirmations

The Ultimate Stop-Loss

- Read morning affirmations aloud
- Visualize successful trading day
- Set positive intentions
- Build confidence and focus

Minutes 11-15: System Review

- Review key trading rules
- Confirm risk management parameters
- Set daily risk limits
- Prepare for market analysis

Minutes 16-20: Market Preparation

- Review overnight news and events
- Check economic calendar
- Identify potential opportunities
- Set realistic expectations

Post-Market Routine (15 minutes)

Minutes 1-5: Trade Review

- Analyze each trade objectively
- Identify rule adherence success
- Note areas for improvement
- Record lessons learned

Minutes 6-10: Emotional Processing

- Acknowledge emotions from day
- Process wins and losses healthily

- Release tension and stress

- Practice gratitude

Minutes 11-15: Affirmations and Planning

- Read evening affirmations

- Visualize tomorrow's success

- Set positive expectations

- End day on constructive note

Tracking Psychological Progress

Mental Performance Metrics

Daily Discipline Score (1-10):

- Rate your rule adherence

- Track improvement over time

- Identify patterns and triggers

- Celebrate progress

Emotional Control Rating (1-10):

- Assess your emotional management

- Note challenging situations

- Practice improvement strategies

- Build emotional resilience

Confidence Level (1-10):

- Monitor confidence trends

- Identify confidence builders/destroyers

- Work on consistent confidence

The Ultimate Stop-Loss

- Maintain realistic self-assessment

Weekly Psychological Review

Questions for Weekly Assessment:

1. How well did I follow my trading rules this week?

2. What emotions challenged me most?

3. Where did I show good discipline?

4. What psychological patterns am I noticing?

5. How can I improve my mental game next week?

Action Items:

- Identify specific areas for improvement

- Plan targeted mental exercises

- Set psychological goals for next week

- Celebrate psychological victories

Advanced Mental Training Techniques

Pressure Training

High-Stress Simulation:

- Practice trading decisions under time pressure

- Use demo account for pressure training

- Simulate large position scenarios

- Build comfort with stress

Benefits:

- Improves decision-making under pressure

- Builds confidence in stressful situations

The Ultimate Stop-Loss

- Reduces anxiety during real trading

- Develops professional composure

Mindfulness Integration

Mindful Trading Practice:

- Stay present during trade analysis

- Notice thoughts without judgment

- Make conscious decisions

- Avoid automatic reactions

Benefits:

- Reduces impulsive decisions

- Improves focus and concentration

- Builds emotional awareness

- Enhances decision quality

Common Psychological Mistakes

Mistake #1: Skipping Mental Preparation

Wrong: Jumping into trading without psychological preparation **Right:** Consistent daily mental routines

Mistake #2: Ignoring Emotions

Wrong: Trying to eliminate all emotions from trading **Right:** Acknowledging and managing emotions effectively

Mistake #3: Perfectionism

Wrong: Expecting to never make mistakes or have losses **Right:** Accepting imperfection while striving for consistency

Mistake #4: Inconsistent Practice

The Ultimate Stop-Loss

Wrong: Only doing mental exercises when feeling bad **Right:** Daily consistent psychological training

Mistake #5: Neglecting Wins

Wrong: Only focusing on mistakes and losses **Right:** Celebrating successes and building on strengths

Chapter 15 Summary: Mental Mastery Keys

Psychological preparation transforms good traders into great ones:

1. **Daily Affirmations:** Consistent positive programming builds profitable habits

2. **Mental Exercises:** Regular psychological training improves performance under pressure

3. **Visualization:** Mental rehearsal creates automatic responses to trading situations

4. **Emotional Management:** Acknowledging and processing emotions prevents poor decisions

5. **Discipline Building:** Mental training strengthens adherence to trading rules

6. **Confidence Development:** Systematic confidence building improves execution quality

Your technical skills are only as good as your ability to execute them consistently under pressure. The mental exercises and affirmations in this chapter provide the psychological foundation for long-term trading success.

Remember: champions in every field dedicate time to mental training. Trading is no different. The time you invest in psychological preparation will pay dividends in improved performance, reduced stress, and greater trading satisfaction.

The Ultimate Stop-Loss

Master your mind, and you'll master the markets. The psychological edge is often the difference between those who dream of trading success and those who achieve it.

Chapter 16: Overcoming the Tight Stop Temptation

"The tight stop is the siren song of amateur traders—it whispers promises of small losses while delivering the certainty of frequent failure. Professional traders resist its call and embrace the wisdom of proper placement."

Introduction: The Most Dangerous Trading Mistake

Every trader faces the temptation to place stops closer than they should. It seems logical—smaller stops mean smaller losses, right? This chapter will expose why tight stops are actually one of the most expensive mistakes in trading and provide you with the psychological and practical tools to overcome this destructive urge.

The tight stop temptation is so powerful because it appears to solve multiple problems: it reduces the fear of large losses, allows for larger position sizes, and makes traders feel more "in control." In reality, tight stops virtually guarantee failure through increased stop-out frequency and poor risk-to-reward ratios.

Understanding and overcoming this temptation is crucial to your success. This chapter will show you why your natural instincts work against you and how to develop the discipline to place stops where they belong—at the last low when buying and last high when selling.

The Psychology Behind Tight Stop Temptation

The Fear-Based Origins

Loss Aversion Bias: Human beings feel losses approximately 2.5 times more intensely than equivalent gains. This evolutionary trait, designed to keep us alive, becomes destructive in trading where small losses are essential for long-term profits.

Tight Stop "Logic":
242

The Ultimate Stop-Loss

- "If I lose less per trade, I'll be more profitable"

- "I can afford larger positions with smaller stops"

- "Small losses don't hurt my account as much"

- "I can be wrong more often and still make money"

The Reality: Tight stops typically result in win rates below 30% and risk-to-reward ratios that make profitability mathematically impossible.

The Control Illusion

False Sense of Security: Tight stops create the illusion that you're "managing risk" when you're actually increasing it. The real risk isn't the size of individual losses—it's the probability of being stopped out before the trade can develop.

Micromanagement Trap: Tight stops encourage obsessive chart watching and second-guessing, leading to emotional decision-making and system abandonment.

The Position Size Temptation

The Math That Deceives:

- 50-pip stop allows 0.2 lots for $100 risk

- 10-pip stop allows 1.0 lot for $100 risk

- The larger position feels more profitable

- Ignores the dramatically reduced success probability

Reality Check: A 1.0 lot position that gets stopped out 80% of the time loses more money than a 0.2 lot position that gets stopped out 40% of the time.

The Mathematical Truth About Tight Stops

Win Rate Destruction

Proper Stop Placement (Last Low/High):

- Typical win rate: 50-60%

The Ultimate Stop-Loss

- Allows trades room to develop

- Respects market volatility

- Provides adequate risk-to-reward ratios

Tight Stop Placement:

- Typical win rate: 20-35%

- Trades stopped out by normal volatility

- Creates need for 3:1+ risk-to-reward just to break even

- Requires 75%+ win rate to be profitable with 1:1 risk-reward

The Profitability Math

Example: 100 Trades with $100 Risk Each

Scenario 1: Proper Stops (30-pip average)

- Win Rate: 55%

- Average Win: $180 (2:1 risk-reward)

- Average Loss: $100

- Result: (55 × $180) - (45 × $100) = $9,900 - $4,500 = $5,400 profit

Scenario 2: Tight Stops (10-pip average)

- Win Rate: 30%

- Average Win: $180 (same profit targets)

- Average Loss: $100

- Result: (30 × $180) - (70 × $100) = $5,400 - $7,000 = -$1,600 loss

Conclusion: Even with identical profit targets, tight stops create guaranteed losses while proper stops generate substantial profits.

The Whipsaw Effect

Definition: Being stopped out of a position just before it moves in your favor.

The Ultimate Stop-Loss

Tight Stop Whipsaw Rate: 60-80% of stopped trades **Proper Stop Whipsaw Rate:** 20-30% of stopped trades

Emotional Damage:

- Watching "your" trade work after being stopped out

- Losing confidence in analysis abilities

- Developing system abandonment tendencies

- Creating revenge trading impulses

Real-World Examples: Tight Stops vs. Proper Placement

Case Study 1: EUR/USD Bullish Engulfing

Market Setup:

- EUR/USD at 1.0950

- Bullish engulfing pattern at support

- Last low at 1.0925 (25 pips below entry)

- Recent volatility: 20-pip average hourly range

Tight Stop Approach:

- Entry: 1.0950

- Stop: 1.0945 (5 pips)

- Position Size: 2.0 lots ($100 risk)

- Outcome: Stopped out within 30 minutes by normal volatility

- Loss: $100

- Trade never had chance to develop

Proper Stop Approach:

- Entry: 1.0950

- Stop: 1.0925 (25 pips, at last low)

The Ultimate Stop-Loss

- Position Size: 0.4 lots ($100 risk)

- Outcome: Initial volatility test to 1.0940, then rally to 1.1000

- Profit: $200 (50-pip gain × 0.4 lots)

- Risk-Reward: 2:1 success

Lesson: The proper stop survived normal market noise and captured the intended move.

Case Study 2: GBP/JPY Bearish Engulfing

Market Setup:

- GBP/JPY at 185.00

- Bearish engulfing at resistance

- Last high at 185.50 (50 pips above entry)

- News event pending in 2 hours

Tight Stop Approach:

- Entry: 185.00

- Stop: 185.15 (15 pips)

- Position Size: 1.33 lots ($200 risk)

- Outcome: Pre-news volatility hits stop at 185.12

- Loss: $200

- News drives pair down 100 pips afterward

Proper Stop Approach:

- Entry: 185.00

- Stop: 185.50 (50 pips, at last high)

- Position Size: 0.4 lots ($200 risk)

- Outcome: Pre-news spike to 185.30, then crash to 183.50

The Ultimate Stop-Loss

- Profit: $600 (150-pip gain × 0.4 lots)

- Risk-Reward: 3:1 success

Lesson: Proper stops account for pre-news volatility and capture full moves.

Case Study 3: USD/CAD Support Test

Market Setup:

- USD/CAD testing major support at 1.3500

- Multiple bounces from this level

- Last low at 1.3480 (20 pips below current price)

- Strong fundamental support for USD

Tight Stop Approach:

- Entry: 1.3500

- Stop: 1.3495 (5 pips below support)

- Reasoning: "Support should hold"

- Position Size: 2.0 lots ($100 risk)

- Outcome: Support tested to 1.3494, stopped out

- Immediate bounce to 1.3550

- Loss: $100 plus psychological damage

Proper Stop Approach:

- Entry: 1.3500

- Stop: 1.3480 (20 pips, at last low)

- Reasoning: "If support breaks significantly, I'm wrong"

- Position Size: 0.5 lots ($100 risk)

- Outcome: Support holds, rally to 1.3580+80 pips gain

The Ultimate Stop-Loss

- Profit: $400

- Confidence in system maintained

Lesson: Support/resistance levels need breathing room for testing.

The Hidden Costs of Tight Stops

Psychological Damage

Confidence Erosion:

- Frequent small losses feel like constant failure

- Doubt in analysis abilities develops

- System abandonment tendencies emerge

- Trading becomes emotionally exhausting

The Frustration Cycle:

1. Place tight stop to "limit risk"

2. Get stopped out by normal volatility

3. Watch trade work afterward

4. Feel frustrated and stupid

5. Try even tighter stops to "improve"

6. Repeat cycle with increasing frustration

Recovery Difficulty: Once caught in the tight stop cycle, traders often need months to rebuild confidence and return to proper placement principles.

Opportunity Cost

Missed Profit Calculation: If tight stops cause you to miss 60% of winning trades that proper stops would capture, your opportunity cost includes:

- Direct profit from missed winning trades

- Compound growth from those profits

The Ultimate Stop-Loss

- Psychological capital from trading confidence

- Time value from extended learning curve

Example:

- Missed trade profit: $500

- Next 10 trades building on that confidence: $2,000

- Total opportunity cost: $2,500 from one tight stop decision

Transaction Cost Multiplication

Increased Trading Frequency: Tight stops lead to more frequent stop-outs, which leads to:

- More re-entry attempts

- Higher spread costs

- Increased slippage

- Greater commission expenses

Cost Comparison:

- Proper stops: 10 trades per month, $50 total costs

- Tight stops: 25 trades per month, $125 total costs

- Additional cost: $75/month = $900/year in unnecessary expenses

Overcoming Tight Stop Psychology: Practical Strategies

Strategy 1: The Volatility Reality Check

Daily Exercise: Before placing any stop, calculate the average hourly range for your timeframe and currency pair over the past 10 days.

Questions to Ask:

- Is my stop distance at least 1.5x the average hourly range?

- Have I accounted for session volatility differences?

The Ultimate Stop-Loss

- Does my stop placement respect recent swing levels?

- Am I placing the stop where I'd be proven wrong, not just uncomfortable?

Reality Grounding: If your stop is closer than recent normal volatility, you're essentially betting against mathematical probability.

Strategy 2: The Position Size Reframe

Mental Shift: Instead of thinking "I can only risk $100, so I need a tight stop to get a decent position size," think "I can risk $100, so let me find the proper stop placement and adjust position size accordingly."

Process:

1. Identify proper stop placement first

2. Calculate required position size for your risk amount

3. Accept the position size as correct for the setup

4. Trust that proper placement will yield better results

Affirmation: "I trade position sizes appropriate for proper stop placement, not stop placement appropriate for desired position sizes."

Strategy 3: The Whipsaw Journal

Daily Tracking: Maintain a record of every trade that gets stopped out with answers to:

- Where was my stop placed?

- What was the distance in pips?

- Did price return to my favor within 4 hours?

- What would have happened with proper placement?

Weekly Review: Calculate your whipsaw percentage and the profit you missed from premature stop-outs.

Goal: Reduce whipsaw rate below 25% through better stop placement.
250

The Ultimate Stop-Loss

Strategy 4: The Patience Meditation

Pre-Trade Meditation (5 minutes):

1. Close your eyes and breathe deeply

2. Visualize the trade developing over hours/days

3. See normal market volatility testing your stop

4. Feel confident in your placement surviving the test

5. Experience the satisfaction of proper execution

Patience Mantras:

- "Good trades need time to develop"

- "Volatility is my friend when I prepare for it"

- "Proper stops separate professionals from amateurs"

Strategy 5: The Mathematical Conviction Exercise

Before Every Trade: Calculate and write down:

- Win rate needed to break even with this stop distance

- Profit potential with proper stop placement

- Historical success rate with similar setups

- Long-term profit expectation

Conviction Builder: When you see that proper stops require only 45% win rate while tight stops need 70%+ win rate, the choice becomes obvious.

The Proper Stop Placement Mindset

Embracing Temporary Discomfort

Professional Perspective: "I place my stops where the market would prove my analysis wrong, not where my emotions feel comfortable."

The Ultimate Stop-Loss

Pain Tolerance Development: Like physical exercise, trading requires tolerance for temporary discomfort (larger individual losses) to achieve long-term benefits (consistent profitability).

Risk vs. Risk Management

True Risk Understanding:

- Risk isn't the size of your stop loss
- Risk is the probability of being wrong
- Tight stops increase probability of being stopped out
- Therefore, tight stops increase real risk

Professional Risk Management: Place stops where they protect against being wrong about market direction, not where they protect against feeling uncomfortable about loss size.

The Confidence Compound Effect

Positive Cycle:

1. Place proper stops based on technical analysis
2. Stops survive normal market volatility
3. More trades reach profit potential
4. Confidence in system grows
5. Easier to place proper stops in future
6. Results continue to improve

Negative Cycle (Tight Stops):

1. Place stops based on comfort, not analysis
2. Normal volatility triggers stops frequently
3. Few trades reach profit potential
4. Confidence in system erodes

The Ultimate Stop-Loss

5. Stops get even tighter to "reduce risk"

6. Results deteriorate further

Advanced Techniques for Stop Discipline

The "Stop Placement Before Entry" Rule

Process:

1. Identify potential setup

2. Determine proper stop placement

3. Calculate position size for your risk amount

4. If position size feels too small, find different setup

5. Never compromise stop placement for position size

Benefits:

- Prevents emotional compromise during trade planning

- Ensures every trade follows proper risk management

- Builds systematic approach to trade selection

The Multiple Timeframe Stop Confirmation

Technique: Before placing any stop, confirm its appropriateness across multiple timeframes:

- 15-minute chart: Is stop beyond recent volatility?

- 1-hour chart: Does stop respect swing structure?

- 4-hour chart: Is stop positioned logically for larger context?

All Three Must Agree: If any timeframe suggests your stop is too tight, adjust placement accordingly.

The News Event Buffer System

The Ultimate Stop-Loss

Standard Stops: Use normal technical placement **Pre-News Stops:** Add 20-30% buffer for volatility spikes **Post-News Stops:** Wait for volatility to settle before trading

Example:

- Normal EUR/USD stop: 25 pips

- Pre-NFP stop: 32 pips (25 + 7 buffer)

- Reasoning: Account for news-driven volatility without abandoning technical principles

Common Tight Stop Justifications (And Why They're Wrong)

Justification 1: "I'm Only Risking Small Amounts"

The Fallacy: Small individual losses from tight stops typically create larger cumulative losses than proper stops due to frequency.

The Reality: 10 small losses of $50 each ($500 total) hurt more than 3 larger losses of $100 each ($300 total), especially when the tight stops prevent you from capturing winning trades.

Justification 2: "I Can Always Re-Enter"

The Fallacy: Getting stopped out and re-entering increases costs and emotional stress while often resulting in worse average prices.

The Reality: Re-entry requires the psychological strength to take the same trade at a worse price after just being stopped out—most traders can't do this consistently.

Justification 3: "Tight Stops Limit My Maximum Loss"

The Fallacy: Tight stops often lead to larger cumulative losses through increased frequency and missed opportunities.

The Reality: Your maximum loss is limited by position sizing, not stop distance. Proper position sizing with proper stops provides better protection.

Justification 4: "The Market Shouldn't Move Against Me That Much"

The Ultimate Stop-Loss

The Fallacy: Markets don't care what you think they "should" do. Normal volatility is a fact, not an opinion.

The Reality: Professional traders adapt to market reality rather than expecting markets to conform to their comfort levels.

Building Long-Term Stop Discipline

The 30-Day Challenge

Week 1-2: Awareness Building

- Track every impulse to tighten stops
- Calculate proper placement before considering position size
- Document emotions around larger stops

Week 3-4: Implementation

- Place all stops at proper technical levels
- Accept smaller position sizes as necessary
- Focus on process over individual trade results

Success Metrics:

- Whipsaw rate below 30%
- Average stop distance matches technical requirements
- Emotional comfort with proper placement

The Annual Review Process

Quarterly Assessment: Compare results from periods of proper stop placement vs. tight stop periods:

- Win rate differences
- Average profit per trade
- Psychological stress levels

- Overall account growth

Yearly Commitment: Pledge to maintain proper stop discipline for entire following year, with quarterly check-ins to ensure compliance.

Chapter 16 Summary: Conquering the Tight Stop Temptation

Overcoming tight stop temptation is essential for trading success:

1. **Psychological Understanding:** Tight stops appeal to loss aversion but guarantee poor results

2. **Mathematical Reality:** Proper stops create better win rates and risk-reward ratios

3. **Opportunity Cost:** Tight stops cause missed profits that dwarf the "saved" losses

4. **Systematic Approach:** Place stops based on technical analysis, not emotional comfort

5. **Long-term Perspective:** Temporary discomfort from proper stops creates lasting profitability

6. **Discipline Development:** Consistent proper placement builds confidence and improves results

The tight stop temptation will always exist—it's part of human psychology. Professional traders succeed by recognizing this urge and systematically overcoming it through proper education, emotional management, and disciplined execution.

Remember: your stops should be placed where the market would prove your analysis wrong, not where your emotions feel comfortable. Master this principle, and you'll overcome one of the most common causes of trading failure.

The market rewards those who give their trades room to develop properly. Embrace proper stop placement, and let your profits run while your discipline protects your capital.

The Ultimate Stop-Loss

Chapter 17: Building Patience and Discipline

"In a world of instant gratification, the patient trader becomes a rare and valuable species. Discipline is not a constraint—it's the foundation of financial freedom."

Introduction: The Twin Pillars of Trading Success

Technical knowledge gets you started, but patience and discipline determine whether you succeed or fail. Chapter 17 will show you how to develop these crucial character traits that separate consistently profitable traders from the majority who struggle.

Patience and discipline work together: patience helps you wait for high-quality setups and let winning trades develop, while discipline ensures you follow your rules even when emotions pull you in different directions. Together, they create the mental framework for long-term success.

The modern world conditions us for instant gratification, making patience and discipline increasingly rare and valuable. Master these traits, and you'll possess advantages that most traders never develop, giving you a significant edge in the markets.

Understanding Trading Patience

The Nature of Market Patience

What Trading Patience IS:

- Waiting for setups that meet your exact criteria

- Allowing winning trades to reach their full potential

- Accepting that good opportunities come in clusters

- Maintaining composure during drawdown periods

- Letting your system work over time

What Trading Patience IS NOT:

The Ultimate Stop-Loss

- Sitting in front of charts all day without trading

- Refusing to exit losing trades hoping they'll turn around

- Waiting for "perfect" setups that never come

- Paralysis analysis leading to missed opportunities

- Passive inaction in the face of changing conditions

The Patience-Profit Connection

High-Quality Setups: Patient traders wait for confluences that dramatically improve win rates:

- Multiple timeframe alignment

- Key support/resistance tests

- Perfect bullish/bearish engulfing patterns

- High-probability news catalysts

- Ideal risk-to-reward scenarios

Example:

- Impatient trader: Takes 20 trades/month, 45% win rate, 1.8:1 R:R

- Patient trader: Takes 8 trades/month, 65% win rate, 2.5:1 R:R

- Result: Patient trader significantly outperforms despite fewer trades

The Compound Effect of Patience

Short-Term Perspective (Impatient):

- Focus on individual trade outcomes

- Frustration with waiting periods

- Overtrading to "make something happen"

- Emotional reactions to market noise

Long-Term Perspective (Patient):

The Ultimate Stop-Loss

- Focus on system performance over time

- Acceptance of natural trading rhythms

- Quality selection creates consistent results

- Emotional stability through market cycles

Understanding Trading Discipline

The Components of Trading Discipline

Rule Adherence: Following your trading system exactly as designed, especially when emotions suggest otherwise.

Risk Management: Never risking more than predetermined amounts, regardless of confidence levels or recent results.

Emotional Control: Making decisions based on analysis rather than fear, greed, hope, or frustration.

Consistency: Applying the same standards and processes to every trading decision.

Self-Accountability: Taking responsibility for results and learning from both successes and failures.

The Discipline-Consistency Loop

Strong Discipline Creates:

- Consistent rule following

- Predictable performance patterns

- Emotional stability

- Confidence in system

- Better long-term results

Weak Discipline Creates:

- Inconsistent execution

The Ultimate Stop-Loss

- Unpredictable results

- Emotional volatility

- System doubt

- Poor long-term performance

The Reinforcing Cycle: Success from discipline builds confidence, making discipline easier to maintain, which creates more success.

The Enemies of Patience and Discipline

Enemy #1: Instant Gratification Culture

Modern Conditioning:

- Social media provides instant feedback

- Technology delivers immediate results

- Consumer culture promises quick solutions

- Entertainment industry offers constant stimulation

Trading Reality:

- Good setups require waiting

- Profits compound over months and years

- Success comes from boring consistency

- Best traders often have quiet, methodical approaches

Counter-Strategy: Deliberately practice delayed gratification in other areas of life to build patience muscles.

Enemy #2: Fear of Missing Out (FOMO)

FOMO Manifestations:

- Taking marginal setups because "something is better than nothing"

- Entering trades late because you watched them develop without acting

The Ultimate Stop-Loss

- Overtrading during active market periods

- Abandoning system when others seem to be making money faster

Anti-FOMO Techniques:

1. **Opportunity Abundance Mindset:** "Markets provide endless opportunities"

2. **Quality Focus:** "I only want trades that meet my standards"

3. **Performance Tracking:** "My best results come from patience"

4. **System Trust:** "My edge comes from selectivity, not frequency"

Enemy #3: Boredom and Understimulation

The Boredom Trap: Markets often provide long periods of choppy, directionless movement that don't offer good trading opportunities. Bored traders often create action where none should exist.

Healthy Boredom Management:

- Develop other interests and hobbies

- Use quiet periods for education and system improvement

- Practice analysis on historical charts

- Maintain fitness and health routines

- Build relationships outside of trading

Enemy #4: Emotional Volatility

High-Emotion Periods:

- After significant wins (overconfidence)

- During losing streaks (desperation)

- Following major news events (excitement/fear)

- At month/quarter end (pressure to perform)

The Ultimate Stop-Loss

Emotional Regulation Strategies:

- Predetermined response protocols

- Cooling-off periods before decisions

- Third-party accountability partners

- Objective performance metrics focus

Building Patience: Practical Exercises

Exercise 1: The Opportunity Journal

Daily Practice: At the end of each trading day, write down:

- How many potential setups you identified

- How many met your exact criteria

- Which ones you took and why

- Which ones you passed on and why

- What you learned about patience that day

Weekly Review: Analyze patterns in your patience levels:

- Which days/times test your patience most?

- What market conditions make you impatient?

- How does patience correlate with your results?

Monthly Goal Setting: Set specific patience goals:

- "I will only take trades that meet all 5 of my criteria"

- "I will wait for at least 3 timeframe confirmations"

- "I will pass on 70% of potential setups"

Exercise 2: The Waiting Meditation

Setup (10 minutes daily):

The Ultimate Stop-Loss

1. Sit comfortably and close your eyes

2. Visualize yourself in front of trading charts

3. See marginal setups appearing

4. Feel the urge to trade something

5. Practice breathing through the urge

6. Visualize waiting for the perfect setup

7. Experience the satisfaction of quality selection

Benefits:

- Builds tolerance for trading inactivity

- Strengthens impulse control

- Creates positive associations with waiting

- Develops patience as an active skill

Exercise 3: The Quality vs. Quantity Tracking

Setup: Create two columns in your trading journal:

- Column 1: Trades that met all criteria (A+ setups)

- Column 2: Trades that met most criteria (B+ setups)

Monthly Analysis: Calculate performance metrics for each category:

- Win rates

- Average profit/loss

- Risk-reward ratios

- Emotional stress levels

Typical Results: A+ trades usually show 15-25% better performance across all metrics, providing mathematical proof that patience pays.

Exercise 4: The Patience Challenge

The Ultimate Stop-Loss

30-Day Challenge Structure:

- Week 1: Only take setups with 4+ confluence factors

- Week 2: Only take setups with 5+ confluence factors

- Week 3: Add minimum 2-hour chart observation before entry

- Week 4: Combine all previous requirements

Success Metrics:

- Number of trades taken (should decrease)

- Win rate percentage (should increase)

- Average profit per trade (should increase)

- Stress levels during trading (should decrease)

Building Discipline: Systematic Approaches

The Rule-Based Trading System

Core Principle: Every trading decision should be based on predetermined rules, not in-the-moment emotions or hunches.

Essential Rules Categories:

Entry Rules:

- Specific pattern requirements (bullish/bearish engulfing)

- Timeframe confirmation requirements

- Volume and momentum criteria

- News event considerations

Stop Loss Rules:

- Last low for buying, last high for selling

- Maximum risk per trade (1% of account)

- No stop adjustments against position

The Ultimate Stop-Loss

- Stop placement before position sizing

Position Sizing Rules:

- Risk percentage per trade

- Maximum position size limits

- Correlation adjustments

- Account size considerations

Exit Rules:

- Profit target calculations

- Trailing stop methodologies

- Time-based exit criteria

- Fundamental change responses

The Pre-Market Discipline Checklist

Daily Preparation (10 minutes):

Mental State Assessment:

- Am I emotionally centered and focused?

- Have I reviewed my trading rules?

- Am I prepared to follow my system exactly?

- Do I have realistic expectations for today?

System Readiness:

- Are my charts configured correctly?

- Have I reviewed overnight news and events?

- Are my risk parameters set properly?

- Do I have my economic calendar updated?

The Ultimate Stop-Loss

Commitment Affirmation:

- I will only take A+ quality setups

- I will risk exactly 1% per trade

- I will place stops at proper technical levels

- I will follow my rules regardless of emotions

The Post-Trade Discipline Review

After Every Trade (5 minutes):

Rule Adherence Check:

- Did I follow my entry criteria exactly?

- Was my stop placed at the proper level?

- Did I size the position according to my rules?

- Was my exit decision systematic or emotional?

Performance Recording:

- Trade outcome (win/loss/breakeven)

- Rule adherence score (1-10)

- Emotional control rating (1-10)

- Lessons learned

Improvement Planning:

- What did I do well?

- Where can I improve discipline?

- What will I focus on in the next trade?

Advanced Patience and Discipline Techniques

The Seasonal Patience Strategy

The Ultimate Stop-Loss

Market Season Recognition:

- **Trending Seasons:** Higher activity, more opportunities

- **Range-Bound Seasons:** Lower activity, patience required

- **News-Heavy Seasons:** Increased volatility, selective approach

- **Holiday Seasons:** Reduced liquidity, minimal activity

Adaptive Patience: Adjust expectations and activity levels based on seasonal patterns:

- Summer: Expect fewer high-quality setups

- Election periods: Focus on post-event opportunities

- Central bank weeks: Prepare for volatility but maintain selectivity

The Discipline Accountability System

Trading Partner Method: Partner with another disciplined trader for mutual accountability:

- Daily check-ins on rule adherence

- Weekly performance reviews

- Monthly goal setting and assessment

- Honest feedback on discipline lapses

Mentor Relationship: Work with an experienced trader who can:

- Provide objective perspective on your discipline

- Share experiences from their development journey

- Offer guidance during challenging periods

- Hold you accountable to your commitments

The Patience Profit Correlation Analysis

The Ultimate Stop-Loss

Monthly Exercise: Create detailed analysis comparing patience levels to profitability:

High Patience Months:

- Number of trades taken

- Win rate achieved

- Average profit per trade

- Stress and satisfaction levels

Low Patience Months:

- Number of trades taken

- Win rate achieved

- Average profit per trade

- Stress and satisfaction levels

Typical Findings: Most traders discover that their highest profit months correlate strongly with their highest patience levels, providing powerful motivation for continued patience development.

The Psychology of Long-Term Development

Patience and Discipline as Investments

Short-Term Costs:

- Missed opportunities that don't meet criteria

- Watching others take trades you passed on

- Feeling "left out" during active markets

- Accepting lower trade frequency

Long-Term Returns:

- Higher win rates from quality selection

The Ultimate Stop-Loss

- Better risk-reward ratios from proper timing

- Reduced stress and emotional volatility

- Sustainable performance that compounds over time

Investment Mindset: "I'm investing current patience to earn future profits and peace of mind."

The Compound Effect of Character Development

Beyond Trading Benefits: Patience and discipline developed through trading improve other life areas:

- Better financial decision-making

- Improved relationships through emotional control

- Enhanced career performance through persistence

- Greater life satisfaction through delayed gratification mastery

Life-Trading Integration:

- Practice patience in daily situations (traffic, lines, delays)

- Apply discipline to health and fitness routines

- Use systematic decision-making in major purchases

- Develop delayed gratification in entertainment and consumption

Common Patience and Discipline Failures

Failure Pattern #1: The Impatience Spiral

Sequence:

1. Miss good setup due to hesitation

2. Feel frustrated about "missed opportunity"

3. Lower standards to catch "next one"

4. Take marginal trade that loses

5. Feel more frustrated and desperate

6. Take even worse trades to "make up" losses

7. Suffer significant drawdown

Prevention:

- Accept that missed opportunities are part of trading

- Maintain systematic approach regardless of recent misses

- Focus on next opportunity rather than dwelling on past

Failure Pattern #2: The Discipline Vacation

Sequence:

1. Experience period of strong discipline and good results

2. Become overconfident in abilities

3. Think "I can relax the rules a little"

4. Start taking shortcuts or exceptions

5. Results deteriorate but attribute to "bad luck"

6. Continue rule violations until major loss occurs

7. Return to discipline after significant damage

Prevention:

- Remember that discipline created the good results

- Never allow "exceptions" to systematic rules

- Treat discipline as non-negotiable regardless of recent success

Failure Pattern #3: The Perfectionism Trap

Sequence:

1. Set unrealistic standards for patience and discipline

The Ultimate Stop-Loss

2. Inevitably fail to meet impossible standards

3. Feel guilty and disappointed in self

4. Abandon systematic approach in frustration

5. Resort to emotional trading and poor decisions

Prevention:

- Set realistic, achievable standards

- Focus on progress rather than perfection

- Allow for human imperfection while maintaining high standards

- Celebrate improvements rather than demanding flawlessness

Measuring Progress in Patience and Discipline

Quantitative Metrics

Patience Measures:

- Average time between trades (should increase with better setups)

- Percentage of identified setups actually taken (should decrease)

- Correlation between setup quality and results (should increase)

- Number of "almost" trades passed on (should increase)

Discipline Measures:

- Rule adherence percentage (target: 95%+)

- Emotional decision frequency (should decrease)

- System deviation incidents (should approach zero)

- Recovery time from discipline lapses (should decrease)

Qualitative Assessments

Weekly Self-Evaluation Questions:

The Ultimate Stop-Loss

1. How patient was I with setup selection this week?

2. Where did I demonstrate good discipline under pressure?

3. What situations tested my patience most?

4. How did I handle emotional challenges to my discipline?

5. What patterns am I noticing in my behavior?

Monthly Character Review:

- Am I becoming more patient over time?

- Is discipline feeling more natural and automatic?

- What triggers still challenge my self-control?

- How has character development affected my results?

The Long-Term Vision: Patience and Discipline as Lifestyle

The Patient Trader's Mindset

Core Beliefs:

- Quality always beats quantity in trading

- The best opportunities come to those who wait

- Discipline creates freedom, not constraint

- Character development is more valuable than quick profits

- Sustainable success requires sustainable habits

Daily Affirmations:

- "I have infinite patience for high-quality opportunities"

- "My discipline is my greatest trading asset"

- "I trust my system and execute with precision"

- "Every moment of patience compounds my future success"

The Ultimate Stop-Loss

Integration with Life Philosophy

Holistic Development: Use trading as a vehicle for character development that enhances all areas of life:

- Professional patience leading to better career decisions

- Personal discipline improving health and relationships

- Financial patience building long-term wealth

- Emotional control enhancing overall life satisfaction

The Ripple Effect: Patience and discipline mastered in trading create positive changes throughout your entire life experience.

Chapter 17 Summary: Mastering the Mental Game

Patience and discipline form the foundation of trading excellence:

1. **Patience Pays:** Quality selection dramatically improves long-term results

2. **Discipline Delivers:** Consistent rule following creates predictable success

3. **Character Investment:** Developing these traits pays dividends beyond trading

4. **Systematic Development:** Use specific exercises and measurements to build these skills

5. **Long-term Perspective:** Focus on character development rather than quick results

6. **Integration Benefits:** Trading patience and discipline enhance all areas of life

The markets reward those who can wait for the right opportunities and execute with unwavering discipline. These are not innate talents—they are learnable skills that improve with deliberate practice and commitment.

The Ultimate Stop-Loss

Remember: in a world of instant gratification, patience becomes a superpower. In markets filled with emotional decisions, discipline becomes your competitive advantage. Master these twin pillars, and you'll join the small percentage of traders who achieve consistent, long-term profitability.

Your technical skills open the door to trading success, but patience and discipline determine whether you walk through it and stay there. Commit to developing these character traits, and watch as your trading—and your life—transform in remarkable ways.

The Ultimate Stop-Loss

ENTRY

BULLISH
ENGULFING

LAST LOW

SL

Chapter 18: Mastery Checklist and Practice Plan

"Mastery is not a destination but a journey of continuous improvement. This checklist is your roadmap to stop loss excellence."

Introduction: Your Path to Stop Loss Mastery

You've learned the technical rules, psychological principles, and practical applications of stop loss mastery. Chapter 18 provides you with a systematic checklist and practice plan to ensure you develop true expertise in these crucial skills.

Mastery doesn't happen overnight—it's built through deliberate practice, consistent application, and continuous refinement. This chapter gives you the structured approach needed to progress from knowledge to expertise to mastery.

Think of this as your personal development curriculum for stop loss excellence. Follow this plan systematically, and you'll build the skills that separate consistently profitable traders from those who struggle.

The Stop Loss Mastery Framework

The Four Levels of Competence

Level 1: Unconscious Incompetence

- Don't know what you don't know
- Place stops randomly or emotionally
- No systematic approach
- Frequent violations of basic principles

Level 2: Conscious Incompetence

- Aware of proper principles but struggle to apply them
- Know stops should be at last low/high but still make mistakes

The Ultimate Stop-Loss

- Recognize poor decisions after making them

- Beginning to track and measure performance

Level 3: Conscious Competence

- Can apply principles correctly with focused effort

- Follow rules consistently when paying attention

- Still requires mental energy and concentration

- Good results when disciplined

Level 4: Unconscious Competence (Mastery)

- Proper stop placement becomes automatic

- No mental energy required for basic decisions

- Intuitive understanding of market context

- Consistent excellence under all conditions

Mastery Development Timeline

Months 1-3: Foundation Building

- Learn and understand core principles

- Practice on demo accounts

- Develop basic discipline

- Build initial confidence

Months 4-6: Skill Development

- Apply principles in live trading

- Refine technique through experience

- Handle various market conditions

- Develop consistency

The Ultimate Stop-Loss

Months 7-12: Competence Building

- Execute with confidence under pressure

- Adapt to different market environments

- Integrate advanced concepts

- Achieve reliable results

Years 2-3: Mastery Achievement

- Automatic execution of principles

- Intuitive market understanding

- Teaching and mentoring capability

- Consistent excellence over time

Comprehensive Mastery Checklist

Technical Knowledge Mastery

Core Principle Understanding:

- I can explain why stops go at last low when buying

- I can explain why stops go at last high when selling

- I understand the primary vs. secondary rule hierarchy

- I can identify bullish and bearish engulfing patterns accurately

- I know when to use bullish engulfing lows as secondary stops

- I know when to use bearish engulfing highs as secondary stops

Chart Analysis Skills:

- I can quickly identify the last low on any timeframe

- I can quickly identify the last high on any timeframe

- I can spot quality bullish engulfing patterns

- I can spot quality bearish engulfing patterns

- I can analyze multiple timeframes for confirmation

- I can adapt analysis to different currency pairs

Market Context Understanding:

- I understand how volatility affects stop placement

- I can adjust for different trading sessions

- I know how news events impact stop reliability

- I can identify when market conditions favor wider stops

- I understand correlation effects on stop placement

Practical Application Mastery

Setup Identification:

- I can identify high-quality buying opportunities

- I can identify high-quality selling opportunities

- I can distinguish between A+ and B+ setups

- I can wait for proper setups without overtrading

- I can pass on marginal opportunities

Stop Placement Execution:

- I place stops at proper levels 95%+ of the time

- I never move stops against my position

- I can place stops quickly without hesitation

- I choose appropriate primary vs. secondary stops

- I remain calm when stops are tested by volatility

Position Management:

The Ultimate Stop-Loss

- I can scale positions while maintaining proper stops

- I can manage multiple positions systematically

- I can trail stops appropriately as trades develop

- I can exit positions according to plan

- I can handle both winning and losing trades professionally

Risk Management Mastery

Position Sizing Excellence:

- I can calculate proper position sizes instantly

- I never risk more than my predetermined amount

- I adjust position sizes based on stop distance

- I account for currency pair differences

- I maintain consistent risk across all trades

Dynamic Risk Adjustment:

- I can adjust risk percentages based on setup quality

- I reduce risk appropriately during drawdowns

- I account for market volatility in risk calculations

- I understand correlation impacts on portfolio risk

- I maintain overall portfolio risk within limits

Account Growth Management:

- I have realistic growth projections

- I track progress against goals systematically

- I can project future account values accurately

- I adjust strategies as account size grows

The Ultimate Stop-Loss

- I balance growth with preservation appropriately

Psychological Mastery

Emotional Control:

- I remain calm when stops are hit

- I don't take losses personally

- I can execute trades under pressure

- I maintain discipline during drawdowns

- I avoid revenge trading after losses

Patience and Discipline:

- I wait for high-quality setups consistently

- I follow my rules even when tempted to deviate

- I resist the urge to place tight stops

- I can sit through periods of no trading opportunities

- I maintain systematic approach regardless of recent results

Confidence and Conviction:

- I trust my analysis and placement decisions

- I can execute trades with conviction

- I maintain confidence during temporary setbacks

- I believe in my long-term success

- I can adapt to changing market conditions

Structured Practice Plan

Phase 1: Foundation Practice (Weeks 1-4)

Week 1: Pattern Recognition Mastery

The Ultimate Stop-Loss

Daily Practice (1 hour):

- Review 50 historical chart examples

- Identify last lows and highs on multiple timeframes

- Mark bullish and bearish engulfing patterns

- Practice proper stop placement on paper

Weekend Review:

- Analyze 100+ patterns across different pairs

- Create personal pattern library with screenshots

- Test pattern recognition speed and accuracy

Week 2: Stop Placement Precision

Daily Practice (1 hour):

- Practice stop placement on 20 different setups

- Calculate position sizes for each placement

- Compare primary vs. secondary stop options

- Time your decision-making process

Weekend Project:

- Create stop placement decision tree

- Build quick reference guide for common scenarios

- Practice placement under simulated time pressure

Week 3: Risk Calculation Fluency

Daily Practice (45 minutes):

- Calculate position sizes for 15 different scenarios

- Practice with various currency pairs

The Ultimate Stop-Loss

- Include different account sizes in calculations

- Build mental math speed and accuracy

Weekend Development:

- Create position sizing templates

- Build Excel calculator for verification

- Practice rapid calculations without tools

Week 4: Integration and Review

Daily Practice (1 hour):

- Combine all skills in complete trade analysis

- Practice entire process from setup to exit

- Time complete analysis workflow

- Identify areas needing improvement

Weekly Assessment:

- Take comprehensive skills test

- Identify remaining weak areas

- Plan specific improvements for Phase 2

Phase 2: Application Practice (Weeks 5-12)

Week 5-6: Demo Trading Implementation

Daily Practice:

- Apply skills in live demo environment

- Take 2-3 demo trades per day

- Focus on process over profits

- Document every decision and outcome

The Ultimate Stop-Loss

Success Metrics:

- 90%+ proper stop placement

- Average 2+ quality setups identified daily

- Consistent position sizing accuracy

- Growing confidence in execution

Week 7-8: Pressure Testing

Daily Practice:

- Trade during news events (demo)

- Practice in high-volatility conditions

- Handle multiple simultaneous positions

- Test psychological limits safely

Skill Development:

- Maintain discipline under pressure

- Execute quickly when needed

- Stay calm during volatile periods

- Build stress tolerance

Week 9-10: Multi-Timeframe Mastery

Daily Practice:

- Analyze setups across 3 timeframes

- Practice timeframe alignment confirmation

- Scale positions using proper stops

- Manage complex position structures

Advanced Skills:

The Ultimate Stop-Loss

- Seamless timeframe analysis

- Confident scaling decisions

- Advanced risk management

- Professional position management

Week 11-12: Real Market Preparation

Daily Practice:

- Final demo trading with real-money psychology

- Practice full trading routine

- Test all systems and procedures

- Build complete confidence

Readiness Assessment:

- Consistent profitable demo results

- Emotional stability under pressure

- Automatic execution of all skills

- Complete system confidence

Phase 3: Live Implementation (Weeks 13-24)

Week 13-16: Careful Live Trading

Implementation Strategy:

- Start with 0.5% risk per trade

- Take only A+ quality setups

- Focus entirely on process

- Ignore short-term P&L fluctuations

Success Metrics:

- Perfect rule adherence

- Emotional stability

- Consistent execution

- Building real-money confidence

Week 17-20: Standard Implementation

Progression Strategy:

- Increase to 1% risk per trade

- Include A and A+ quality setups

- Begin scaling selected positions

- Track all performance metrics

Development Goals:

- Natural execution under real conditions

- Profitable performance trending

- Confidence in live environment

- Systematic continuous improvement

Week 21-24: Advanced Implementation

Mastery Demonstration:

- Full risk implementation (1-2%)

- Complex position management

- Advanced scaling strategies

- Teaching others your methods

Mastery Indicators:

- Automatic correct decisions

The Ultimate Stop-Loss

- Consistent profitable results

- Emotional mastery

- Leadership capability

Phase 4: Mastery Maintenance (Ongoing)

Monthly Skills Review:

- Assess all checklist items

- Practice weak areas specifically

- Challenge skills in new contexts

- Maintain sharp execution

Quarterly System Evolution:

- Review and update methods

- Incorporate new market insights

- Refine based on experience

- Stay current with best practices

Annual Mastery Assessment:

- Complete comprehensive evaluation

- Compare to mastery standards

- Plan continued development

- Consider teaching/mentoring roles

Practice Exercises by Skill Level

Beginner Exercises (Months 1-3)

Exercise 1: Pattern Library Building Create a library of 500+ screenshots showing:

- Perfect bullish engulfing patterns

- Perfect bearish engulfing patterns

- Clear last low examples

- Clear last high examples

- Both strong and weak pattern examples

Exercise 2: Stop Placement Speed Drills Time yourself placing stops on 20 different setups:

- Target: Under 30 seconds per placement

- Include position size calculation

- Practice with various currency pairs

- Build automatic response patterns

Exercise 3: Paper Trading Marathon Complete 100 paper trades focusing on:

- Perfect rule adherence

- Detailed documentation

- Process over profits

- Building confidence

Intermediate Exercises (Months 4-9)

Exercise 1: Multi-Timeframe Analysis Practice analyzing 50 setups across 3 timeframes:

- Identify bias on higher timeframe

- Find setup on entry timeframe

- Confirm with lower timeframe

- Document confluence factors

Exercise 2: Volatility Adaptation Practice Practice stop placement in various conditions:

The Ultimate Stop-Loss

- High volatility periods (news events)

- Low volatility periods (holiday trading)

- Session transition times

- Different currency pair characteristics

Exercise 3: Scaling Simulation Practice 25 scaling scenarios:

- 2-position scales

- 3-position scales

- Progressive stop management

- Risk allocation calculations

Advanced Exercises (Months 10-18)

Exercise 1: Pressure Training Simulate high-stress trading conditions:

- Time-pressured decisions

- Large position management

- Multiple simultaneous trades

- High-stakes psychological pressure

Exercise 2: Teaching Preparation Explain concepts to others:

- Write detailed explanations

- Create educational materials

- Mentor beginning traders

- Develop training programs

Exercise 3: System Innovation Develop improvements to basic methods:

- Research new applications

- Test refinements carefully

- Document improvements

- Share with trading community

Daily Practice Routines

Morning Preparation Routine (15 minutes)

Minutes 1-3: Skills Affirmation

- "I place stops at last lows when buying"

- "I place stops at last highs when selling"

- "I calculate position sizes precisely"

- "I execute with discipline and confidence"

Minutes 4-8: Chart Review

- Scan major pairs for setup opportunities

- Identify proper stop placements

- Calculate preliminary position sizes

- Note market conditions

Minutes 9-12: Economic Calendar Check

- Review day's news events

- Plan risk adjustments if needed

- Identify high-volatility periods

- Prepare contingency plans

Minutes 13-15: Intention Setting

- Set specific goals for the day

- Commit to rule adherence

- Prepare mentally for challenges

The Ultimate Stop-Loss

- Visualize successful execution

Evening Review Routine (20 minutes)

Minutes 1-5: Trade Analysis

- Review each trade taken

- Assess rule adherence

- Calculate performance metrics

- Identify improvement areas

Minutes 6-10: Skills Assessment

- Rate stop placement accuracy

- Evaluate position sizing precision

- Assess emotional control

- Note psychological challenges

Minutes 11-15: Practice Planning

- Plan tomorrow's practice focus

- Set specific skill goals

- Prepare challenging scenarios

- Schedule skill development time

Minutes 16-20: Knowledge Building

- Read trading education materials

- Study market analysis

- Research new techniques

- Build theoretical understanding

Progress Tracking Systems

The Ultimate Stop-Loss

Weekly Skills Scorecard

Technical Skills (40 points maximum):

- Stop placement accuracy (10 points)

- Position sizing precision (10 points)

- Pattern recognition speed (10 points)

- Multi-timeframe analysis (10 points)

Execution Skills (30 points maximum):

- Rule adherence percentage (15 points)

- Decision-making speed (10 points)

- Trade management quality (5 points)

Psychological Skills (30 points maximum):

- Emotional control (15 points)

- Patience and discipline (10 points)

- Confidence levels (5 points)

Total Score Interpretation:

- 90-100: Mastery level performance

- 80-89: Advanced competence

- 70-79: Intermediate competence

- 60-69: Developing competence

- Below 60: Needs focused improvement

Monthly Progress Assessment

Quantitative Measures:

- Trades taken vs. opportunities identified

The Ultimate Stop-Loss

- Win rate compared to historical average

- Average risk-reward ratio achieved

- Rule violation frequency

- Position sizing accuracy percentage

Qualitative Measures:

- Confidence level in execution

- Emotional stability during trading

- Patience with setup selection

- Discipline under pressure

- Teaching ability to others

Development Planning: Based on assessment results, create specific plans for:

- Weak areas requiring focus

- Strengths to leverage further

- New challenges to undertake

- Advanced skills to develop

Chapter 18 Summary: Your Mastery Journey

Stop loss mastery is achieved through systematic development:

1. **Progressive Learning:** Move through competence levels systematically

2. **Comprehensive Checklist:** Master all aspects of technical and psychological skills

3. **Structured Practice:** Follow proven development phases

4. **Daily Routines:** Build skills through consistent daily practice

The Ultimate Stop-Loss

5. **Progress Tracking:** Measure improvement objectively

6. **Continuous Development:** Maintain and evolve skills over time

Mastery is not a destination but a journey of continuous improvement. This checklist and practice plan provide your roadmap, but your commitment and consistent effort will determine how quickly you progress.

Remember: every expert was once a beginner. Every master was once a disaster. Your current skill level doesn't matter—what matters is your commitment to systematic improvement using the tools provided in this chapter.

Start where you are, use what you have, do what you can. Follow this plan consistently, and you'll develop the stop loss mastery that creates long-term trading success.

Chapter 19: Connecting to Your Trading System

"Stop loss mastery is not a standalone skill—it's the foundation that makes every other trading technique more effective. Integration creates exponential improvement."

Introduction: The Integration Imperative

You've mastered stop loss placement as an isolated skill, but true trading success comes from integrating these principles into a complete trading system. Chapter 19 shows you how to connect your stop loss mastery to every other aspect of your trading approach.

Integration is where individual skills become exponentially more powerful. Your stop loss mastery will enhance your entry timing, improve your position sizing, strengthen your risk management, and increase your overall profitability.

This chapter provides specific guidance for integrating stop loss principles with popular trading methodologies, ensuring that regardless of your preferred approach, you'll maximize the benefits of proper stop placement.

The Foundation Principle: Stops First, Everything Else Second

The Traditional (Wrong) Approach

Typical Trader Thought Process:

1. "I like this setup, I want to trade it"

2. "I'll risk $100 on this trade"

3. "Where can I put my stop to make the math work?"

4. "I'll place it here, close enough to my entry"

Result: Stops placed for convenience rather than technical validity, leading to frequent stop-outs and poor performance.

The Mastery Approach

The Ultimate Stop-Loss

Professional Trader Thought Process:

1. "I see a potential setup forming"

2. "Where would my stop need to go if I traded this?"

3. "Is the stop placement technically sound?"

4. "What position size gives me proper risk for this stop distance?"

5. "Does the risk-reward justify taking this trade?"

Result: Every trade starts with technically valid stop placement, dramatically improving success rates.

The Integration Mindset

Core Principle: Your stop loss placement should drive position sizing, not the other way around.

Implementation: Before considering any trade, identify where your stop would go using proper principles. Only then calculate position size and evaluate opportunity attractiveness.

Benefits:

- Dramatically higher success rates

- Emotionally easier trade management

- Reduced psychological stress

- More consistent long-term results

Integrating with Technical Analysis Systems

Moving Average Systems

Common Integration Points:

Trend Following with Moving Averages:

- Use moving averages to identify trend direction

- Wait for pullbacks to moving average support/resistance

The Ultimate Stop-Loss

- Apply stop loss rules to pullback patterns

- Place stops at last low/high, not at moving average level

Enhanced Integration Example:

- 200 EMA shows uptrend in EUR/USD

- Price pulls back to test 50 EMA support

- Bullish engulfing pattern forms at 50 EMA

- Stop goes at last low (not at 50 EMA)

- Position sized based on stop distance

Benefits of Proper Integration:

- Moving averages provide context and timing

- Stop loss rules provide precise exit levels

- Combination creates robust entry/exit methodology

Support and Resistance Systems

Traditional Approach Problems:

- Stops placed just below support levels

- Stops placed just above resistance levels

- Frequent stop-outs from support/resistance testing

- Poor risk-reward ratios

Integrated Mastery Approach:

- Use support/resistance for setup identification

- Apply stop loss rules for placement decisions

- Stops go at last low/high, which may be beyond support/resistance

- Better survival rates during level testing

The Ultimate Stop-Loss

Example Integration: EUR/USD testing major support at 1.0900:

- Traditional: Stop at 1.0895 (just below support)

- Mastery: Stop at 1.0875 (last low on relevant timeframe)

- Result: Position survives support testing and captures rebound

Fibonacci Systems

Integration Points:

Fibonacci Retracement Trading:

- Use Fibonacci levels to identify potential reversal zones

- Wait for bullish/bearish engulfing patterns at key levels

- Apply stop loss rules rather than Fibonacci-based stops

- Position size based on technical stop distance

Example:

- EUR/USD retraces to 61.8% Fibonacci level

- Bullish engulfing pattern forms at this level

- Stop placed at last low (not at next Fibonacci level)

- Position sized for stop distance, not Fibonacci targets

Enhanced Performance:

- Fibonacci provides high-probability reversal zones

- Stop loss mastery provides reliable exit methodology

- Integration improves both entry timing and risk management

Candlestick Pattern Systems

Natural Integration: Your stop loss mastery naturally integrates with candlestick analysis:

Enhanced Pattern Trading:

299

The Ultimate Stop-Loss

- Identify bullish/bearish engulfing patterns

- Confirm with additional candlestick signals

- Apply stop loss rules for placement

- Size positions based on technical stop requirements

Advanced Integration Example:

- Morning star pattern forms at support

- Bullish engulfing confirms reversal

- Stop placed at last low (incorporating pattern context)

- Multiple confirmation signals increase confidence

Integrating with Fundamental Analysis

News-Based Trading Integration

Enhanced News Trading:

- Fundamental analysis identifies potential catalysts

- Technical analysis times entries around news

- Stop loss mastery provides risk management

- Integration creates comprehensive approach

Example Integration:

- Fundamental analysis suggests USD strength

- EUR/USD forms bearish engulfing after poor EUR data

- Stop placed at last high using technical rules

- Position sized for technical stop distance

Benefits:

- Fundamental bias improves directional accuracy

The Ultimate Stop-Loss

- Technical timing improves entry precision

- Stop loss mastery ensures proper risk management

Economic Indicator Integration

Systematic Approach:

1. **Pre-Release:** Identify potential trading scenarios

2. **Post-Release:** Apply technical analysis to resulting price action

3. **Entry Execution:** Use stop loss rules for all positions

4. **Risk Management:** Size positions based on technical stops

Example Workflow:

- NFP release expected to be strong

- Plan to buy USD/JPY if data beats expectations

- News confirms strength, USD/JPY rallies

- Wait for pullback and bullish engulfing pattern

- Enter with stop at last low, not news-based level

Integrating with Different Trading Styles

Scalping Integration

Scalping Challenges:

- Very short timeframes

- Tight profit targets

- Quick decision requirements

- High frequency trading

Integration Solutions:

- Apply stop loss rules to 1-minute charts

The Ultimate Stop-Loss

- Use bullish/bearish engulfing on micro timeframes

- Maintain proper stop placement despite quick targets

- Scale position sizes for very tight stops when appropriate

Scalping Example:

- 1-minute EUR/USD bullish engulfing at support

- Stop at last low on 1-minute chart (3-5 pips)

- Large position size due to tight stop

- Quick profit target (5-8 pips)

- Maintains proper risk-reward despite short timeframe

Day Trading Integration

Day Trading Advantages:

- Intraday timeframes suit stop loss principles perfectly

- Multiple opportunities for pattern recognition

- Clear session-based analysis

- Reduced overnight risk

Integration Approach:

- Use 5-minute and 15-minute charts for setup identification

- Apply stop loss rules to chosen timeframe

- Incorporate session characteristics into analysis

- Scale positions appropriately for intraday volatility

Day Trading Example:

- 15-minute GBP/USD bearish engulfing at London open

- Stop at last high on 15-minute chart

The Ultimate Stop-Loss

- Position sized for 15-minute stop distance

- Target based on session average ranges

- Clear rules for all decision points

Swing Trading Integration

Swing Trading Benefits:

- Longer timeframes reduce noise impact

- Better development time for patterns

- Larger profit targets justify wider stops

- More time for analysis and decision-making

Integration Strategy:

- Use 1-hour and 4-hour charts for analysis

- Apply stop loss rules to swing timeframes

- Account for overnight and weekend gaps

- Build positions over multiple sessions

Swing Trading Example:

- Daily EUR/USD bullish engulfing at major support

- Stop at last low on daily chart

- Position sized for daily timeframe stop

- Target based on weekly resistance levels

- Hold through normal intraday volatility

Position Trading Integration

Position Trading Characteristics:

- Weekly and monthly chart analysis

The Ultimate Stop-Loss

- Fundamental factors heavily weighted

- Long holding periods

- Large profit potential

Integration Methodology:

- Apply stop loss rules to weekly charts

- Account for fundamental shifts in placement

- Size positions for very wide stops

- Maintain technical discipline despite long timeframes

Position Trading Example:

- Monthly USD/JPY bullish engulfing at major support

- Stop at last low on monthly chart (very wide)

- Small position size due to wide stop

- Target based on long-term fundamental factors

- Hold through multiple cycles

Creating Your Integrated Trading Plan

Step 1: Define Your Core Methodology

Questions to Answer:

- What is your primary analysis method? (Technical, Fundamental, Combined)

- What timeframes do you prefer to trade?

- What trading style suits your personality and schedule?

- What market conditions do you trade best?

Integration Planning: Document how stop loss principles will enhance your chosen methodology without replacing its core logic.

The Ultimate Stop-Loss

Step 2: Establish Integration Rules

Technical Integration Rules:

- Stops always placed using last low/high principles

- Position sizes always calculated based on stop distance

- No exceptions for "special" setups or market conditions

- Stop placement confirmed before position sizing

Fundamental Integration Rules:

- Fundamental analysis provides bias and timing

- Technical analysis provides precise entry and exit levels

- Stop loss mastery governs all risk management decisions

- Fundamental changes may trigger early exits but not stop movement

Step 3: Build Decision Hierarchies

Decision Priority Order:

1. **Market Analysis:** Is there a tradeable opportunity?

2. **Setup Confirmation:** Does it meet your methodology criteria?

3. **Stop Placement:** Where would stops go using proper principles?

4. **Risk Assessment:** Is the risk-reward acceptable?

5. **Position Sizing:** What size provides proper risk?

6. **Execution:** Enter trade with predetermined plan

The Ultimate Stop-Loss

Example Decision Tree:

Setup Identified → Stop Placement Valid? → Risk-Reward Good? → Position Size Calculated → Trade Executed

↓	↓	↓	↓	↓
Yes	Yes	Yes	Yes	Success
↓	↓	↓	↓	
No	No	No	No	
↓	↓	↓	↓	
Pass on Trade	Pass on Trade	Pass on Trade	Adjust or Pass	

Step 4: Create Integration Workflows

Daily Workflow Example:

1. **Morning Analysis (30 minutes):**

   o   Scan for setups using primary methodology

   o   Identify proper stop placements for each

   o   Calculate position sizes and risk-rewards

   o   Prioritize opportunities

2. **Trading Session (Variable):**

   o   Execute planned trades using integrated approach

   o   Monitor positions according to predetermined rules

   o   Apply stop loss principles to all management decisions

   o   Document all decisions and outcomes

3. **Evening Review (15 minutes):**

   o   Assess integration effectiveness

   o   Identify improvement opportunities

- o Plan next day's focus areas

- o Update integration rules if needed

Integration Success Metrics

Performance Measurement

Traditional Metrics:

- Win rate percentage

- Average profit per trade

- Maximum drawdown

- Sharpe ratio

Integration-Specific Metrics:

- Stop placement accuracy (should be 95%+)

- Whipsaw rate (should be under 25%)

- Risk-reward achievement (should meet targets)

- System adherence percentage (should be 90%+)

Integration Quality Assessment

Monthly Evaluation Questions:

1. Are my stops being placed using proper principles consistently?

2. Is my position sizing driven by stop placement or other factors?

3. How well are my primary methodology and stop loss mastery working together?

4. What integration challenges am I facing repeatedly?

5. Where can I improve the integration further?

Continuous Improvement Process

Quarterly Integration Review:

The Ultimate Stop-Loss

- Analyze performance with and without proper integration

- Identify specific areas where integration breaks down

- Develop solutions for common integration challenges

- Update integration rules based on experience

Annual System Evolution:

- Major review of entire integrated approach

- Consider changes to primary methodology

- Assess stop loss mastery development

- Plan next year's integration improvements

Common Integration Mistakes

Mistake #1: Methodology Override

Wrong: "This is such a good setup, I'll place my stop closer than the last low"
Right: "If the proper stop placement doesn't provide good risk-reward, I'll pass on this setup"

Mistake #2: Position Size Priority

Wrong: "I want to risk $200, so I'll adjust my stop to make the math work"
Right: "My stop goes at the last low, so I'll calculate position size based on that distance"

Mistake #3: Selective Application

Wrong: Using proper stops only on some trades based on "confidence levels"
Right: Applying stop loss principles to every single trade without exception

Mistake #4: Methodology Confusion

Wrong: Trying to integrate too many different approaches simultaneously
Right: Master integration with one primary methodology before adding complexity

Mistake #5: Integration Abandonment

The Ultimate Stop-Loss

Wrong: Reverting to old habits during stressful periods **Right:** Maintaining integration discipline especially during challenging times

Advanced Integration Concepts

Multi-System Integration

For Experienced Traders:

- Integrate stop loss mastery with multiple trading methodologies
- Use different approaches for different market conditions
- Maintain consistent stop loss principles across all systems
- Scale complexity gradually based on mastery level

Portfolio Integration

Portfolio-Level Considerations:

- Apply stop loss principles to overall portfolio risk
- Consider correlation effects in stop placement
- Scale individual position risks based on portfolio exposure
- Maintain overall risk limits regardless of individual opportunities

Automation Integration

Technology Enhancement:

- Use alerts for setup identification
- Automate position size calculations
- Create templates for integrated decision-making
- Maintain human oversight of all critical decisions

Chapter 19 Summary: Integration Excellence

Connecting stop loss mastery to your trading system creates exponential improvement:

The Ultimate Stop-Loss

1. **Foundation First:** Always determine stop placement before position sizing

2. **Enhanced Performance:** Integration improves every aspect of your trading

3. **Systematic Approach:** Create clear workflows and decision hierarchies

4. **Consistent Application:** Apply principles to every trade without exception

5. **Continuous Improvement:** Regularly assess and enhance integration effectiveness

6. **Avoid Common Mistakes:** Maintain discipline especially during challenging periods

Your stop loss mastery is not complete until it's fully integrated with your overall trading approach. This integration is where individual skills become a powerful, cohesive system capable of generating consistent long-term profits.

Remember: great traders are not those with the most complex systems, but those who execute simple, proven principles with unwavering consistency. Your stop loss mastery provides the foundation—proper integration makes it unstoppable.

Take the time to thoughtfully integrate these principles with your chosen methodology. The effort you invest in integration will pay dividends in improved performance, reduced stress, and greater trading satisfaction for years to come.

Chapter 20: Final Success Principles

"Mastery is not the end of the journey—it's the beginning of a new level of responsibility. With great power comes the obligation to use it wisely, share it generously, and build upon it continuously."

Introduction: Your Transformation Complete

You began this journey learning basic stop loss placement. You're ending it with mastery of one of trading's most critical skills. Chapter 20 consolidates everything you've learned into final success principles that will guide you throughout your trading career.

This isn't just the end of a book—it's the beginning of your new identity as a trader who possesses genuine expertise in risk management. The principles in this final chapter will serve as your compass when markets challenge you, your foundation when uncertainty arises, and your legacy when you eventually teach others.

Success in trading, like success in life, comes down to consistently applying proven principles regardless of circumstances. These final principles represent the distilled wisdom of your entire stop loss mastery journey.

The Ten Commandments of Stop Loss Mastery

Commandment I: Thou Shalt Place Stops at the Last Low When Buying

The Eternal Truth: No matter how markets evolve, how technology advances, or how your experience grows, this principle remains constant. The last low represents the market's most recent statement of where buyers were willing to step in. Respect this wisdom.

Application:

- Before considering any buying opportunity, identify the last low
- Place your stop at this level without compromise
- Trust this placement over your emotions or hunches

The Ultimate Stop-Loss

- Remember: this is where the market has already voted

Life Application: Just as in trading, life's best decisions often come from respecting proven patterns rather than fighting them.

Commandment II: Thou Shalt Place Stops at the Last High When Selling

The Mirror Truth: The counterpart to Commandment I, equally sacred and inviolable. The last high shows where sellers last overwhelmed buyers. Honor this information.

Application:

- Every selling opportunity requires identifying the last high

- Your stop belongs at this level, period

- Ignore the temptation to place it closer

- Trust the market's demonstrated resistance level

Universal Principle: Success comes from working with natural forces rather than against them.

Commandment III: Thou Shalt Never Move Stops Against Thy Position

The Discipline Covenant: Once placed, stops are sacred boundaries. Moving them against your position breaks the fundamental contract of risk management and opens the door to unlimited losses.

Application:

- Set your stop and consider it immutable

- Moving stops closer to breakeven or profit is acceptable

- Moving stops further from entry is forbidden

- Your initial analysis was done calmly—trust it

Character Building: This discipline builds the strength of character needed for all life challenges.

Commandment IV: Thou Shalt Size Positions Based on Stop Distance

The Ultimate Stop-Loss

The Mathematical Law: Your position size must be determined by your stop distance and risk amount, never by greed, fear, or arbitrary preferences.

Application:

- Calculate position size: Risk Amount ÷ (Stop Distance × Pip Value)

- Accept whatever position size this calculation provides

- Never adjust stops to accommodate desired position sizes

- Mathematics, not emotions, determines your exposure

Financial Wisdom: This principle extends to all financial decisions—risk management drives allocation.

Commandment V: Thou Shalt Risk Only What Thou Can Afford to Lose

The Foundation Stone: Every trade must be sized so that its loss won't materially impact your account or psychology. This enables clear thinking and proper execution.

Application:

- Never risk more than 1-2% of your account on any single trade

- Ensure trade losses won't affect your living expenses

- Size trades so you can sleep peacefully regardless of outcome

- Remember: protecting capital is more important than making profits

Life Lesson: True wealth comes from preservation and steady growth, not spectacular gains.

Commandment VI: Thou Shalt Be Patient and Wait for Quality

The Virtue of Waiting: The market rewards those who wait for high-probability opportunities rather than those who act on every possibility.

Application:

- Pass on 70%+ of potential setups

The Ultimate Stop-Loss

- Wait for multiple timeframe confirmations

- Require clear bullish/bearish engulfing patterns

- Accept that great opportunities are worth waiting for

Success Philosophy: Excellence in any field comes from selective focus on the highest-quality opportunities.

Commandment VII: Thou Shalt Maintain Discipline Under All Conditions

The Consistency Imperative: Your rules must be followed regardless of recent results, market conditions, or emotional states. Consistency creates predictable success.

Application:

- Follow your system during winning streaks

- Follow your system during losing streaks

- Apply rules equally to all market conditions

- Never make exceptions for "special" circumstances

Character Development: Discipline in trading builds discipline in all areas of life.

Commandment VIII: Thou Shalt Learn from Every Trade

The Growth Mindset: Each trade, whether winning or losing, contains lessons that improve your future performance. Embrace this continuous learning process.

Application:

- Review every trade for lesson extraction

- Document what worked and what didn't

- Identify patterns in your decision-making

- Continuously refine your approach based on experience

The Ultimate Stop-Loss

Lifelong Learning: The commitment to continuous improvement ensures you never stop growing.

Commandment IX: Thou Shalt Share Thy Knowledge Generously

The Teaching Obligation: Once you've mastered these principles, you have a responsibility to help others learn them. Teaching reinforces your own understanding while helping others succeed.

Application:

- Mentor new traders in proper risk management

- Share your experiences honestly and openly

- Create educational content when possible

- Build a community of disciplined traders

Legacy Building: Your greatest contribution may be the traders you help develop.

Commandment X: Thou Shalt Never Stop Growing

The Mastery Mindset: Mastery is not a destination but a continuous journey. Stay humble, keep learning, and always seek to improve your craft.

Application:

- Study markets continuously throughout your career

- Adapt techniques as markets evolve

- Challenge yourself with new applications

- Remain open to better methods while maintaining core principles

Life Philosophy: The moment you stop growing is the moment you start declining.

The Success Hierarchy: Building Your Trading Empire

Level 1: Personal Mastery (Months 1-12)

The Ultimate Stop-Loss

Focus: Developing individual competence **Goals:**

- Master stop placement techniques

- Build consistent discipline

- Achieve profitable performance

- Develop emotional control

Success Metrics:

- 95%+ proper stop placement

- Consistent monthly profitability

- Emotional stability during drawdowns

- Growing account balance

Level 2: System Optimization (Year 2-3)

Focus: Refining and perfecting your approach **Goals:**

- Optimize risk-reward ratios

- Develop advanced scaling techniques

- Master multiple timeframe analysis

- Build systematic excellence

Success Metrics:

- Sharpe ratio above 2.0

- Maximum drawdown under 15%

- Consistent outperformance of benchmarks

- Systematic approach to all decisions

Level 3: Wealth Building (Year 3-5)

Focus: Scaling success into significant wealth **Goals:**

The Ultimate Stop-Loss

- Generate substantial monthly income

- Build investment-grade performance record

- Develop multiple income streams

- Achieve financial independence

Success Metrics:

- Account values supporting desired lifestyle

- Consistent income generation

- Diversified wealth building

- Financial security achieved

Level 4: Legacy Creation (Year 5+)

Focus: Teaching, mentoring, and contributing to the trading community
Goals:

- Mentor other traders

- Create educational content

- Build trading-related businesses

- Leave lasting positive impact

Success Metrics:

- Students achieving profitable performance

- Recognition as expert in field

- Contribution to trading knowledge

- Positive impact on trading community

The Character Traits of Successful Traders

Patience: The Strategic Advantage

Development:

The Ultimate Stop-Loss

- Practice delayed gratification in daily life

- Celebrate quality over quantity in all endeavors

- Build tolerance for uncertainty and waiting

- Focus on long-term results over short-term excitement

Trading Application:

- Wait for A+ setups consistently

- Allow winning trades to develop fully

- Accept periods of low activity

- Maintain perspective during drawdowns

Discipline: The Execution Engine

Development:

- Follow routines consistently in all areas of life

- Make commitments and honor them completely

- Practice self-control in challenging situations

- Build systematic approaches to important decisions

Trading Application:

- Follow trading rules without exception

- Maintain risk management discipline

- Execute trades according to plan

- Stay systematic under pressure

Humility: The Learning Accelerator

Development:

- Acknowledge what you don't know

The Ultimate Stop-Loss

- Seek feedback and guidance actively

- Learn from mistakes without defensiveness

- Respect market forces and other successful traders

Trading Application:

- Accept losses as part of the business

- Continuously study and improve

- Respect market volatility and uncertainty

- Learn from both wins and losses

Resilience: The Comeback Power

Development:

- Build tolerance for temporary setbacks

- Develop recovery strategies for difficult periods

- Maintain optimism through challenges

- Focus on solutions rather than problems

Trading Application:

- Recover quickly from losing trades

- Maintain confidence during drawdowns

- Adapt to changing market conditions

- Stay committed to long-term success

Integrity: The Foundation Stone

Development:

- Be honest with yourself about performance

- Take responsibility for all results

The Ultimate Stop-Loss

- Keep commitments to yourself and others

- Maintain ethical standards in all dealings

Trading Application:

- Honest performance analysis and reporting

- Responsibility for all trading decisions

- Ethical approach to trading and teaching

- Authentic representation of results and methods

The Wealth Mindset: Beyond Trading Success

Viewing Trading as Business

Business Principles:

- Treat trading as a professional business operation

- Maintain proper records and accounting

- Reinvest profits for growth when appropriate

- Diversify income streams as success grows

Professional Standards:

- Set business hours and stick to them

- Maintain professional workspace and equipment

- Continue education and skill development

- Network with other professional traders

Building Multiple Income Streams

Direct Trading Income:

- Personal account management

- Proprietary trading firm participation

- Performance-based compensation structures

Indirect Trading Income:

- Teaching and mentoring services

- Educational content creation

- Trading system development

- Consultation and advisory services

Investment Income:

- Real estate investments funded by trading profits

- Stock market investments using trading skills

- Business ownership and entrepreneurship

- Alternative investments and asset classes

Legacy and Impact Considerations

Personal Legacy:

- The traders you've helped develop

- The knowledge you've shared

- The positive impact on the trading community

- The example you've set for others

Financial Legacy:

- Wealth created through disciplined trading

- Investments made with trading profits

- Security provided for family

- Charitable contributions and community impact

The Future of Stop Loss Mastery

The Ultimate Stop-Loss

Evolving Market Conditions

Technological Changes:

- Algorithmic trading increasing market efficiency

- Faster execution speeds and tighter spreads

- New currency pairs and trading instruments

- Enhanced analysis tools and platforms

Adapting Core Principles:

- Stop placement rules remain constant

- Application methods may evolve with technology

- Risk management principles become more important

- Human psychology remains the same

Teaching the Next Generation

Your Responsibility: As you achieve mastery, you have an obligation to help others learn these principles:

Teaching Methods:

- One-on-one mentoring relationships

- Group education and workshops

- Written content and educational materials

- Video content and online courses

Key Messages to Share:

- Stop loss mastery is learnable by anyone

- Patience and discipline can be developed

- Risk management is more important than market analysis

- Long-term consistency beats short-term brilliance

Continuous Innovation

Areas for Development:

- New applications of stop loss principles

- Integration with emerging trading technologies

- Enhanced risk management techniques

- Improved teaching and learning methods

Innovation Principles:

- Build upon core principles rather than replacing them

- Test new methods carefully before full implementation

- Share discoveries with the trading community

- Maintain focus on practical application

Your Personal Trading Constitution

Create Your Trading Mission Statement

Template: "I am a disciplined trader who places stops at the last low when buying and last high when selling. I risk only what I can afford to lose, size positions based on stop distance, and maintain unwavering discipline under all market conditions. I will continuously learn, share my knowledge generously, and build lasting wealth through consistent application of proven principles."

Customize for Your Situation:

- Add your specific goals and timeline

- Include your preferred trading style and markets

- Incorporate your teaching and mentoring commitments

- Reflect your personal values and priorities

Create Your Trading Bill of Rights

The Ultimate Stop-Loss

Your Rights as a Master Trader:

1. The right to take only high-quality setups that meet your criteria

2. The right to place stops where technical analysis dictates

3. The right to risk only amounts that don't affect your peace of mind

4. The right to pass on opportunities that don't meet your standards

5. The right to make mistakes and learn from them

6. The right to take breaks when needed for mental health

7. The right to evolve your methods based on experience

8. The right to teach others what you've learned

9. The right to enjoy the fruits of your disciplined approach

10. The right to be proud of your mastery achievement

Create Your Trading Responsibilities Pledge

Your Responsibilities as a Master Trader:

1. To follow stop loss principles without exception

2. To maintain disciplined risk management at all times

3. To continue learning and improving throughout your career

4. To share knowledge and help other traders develop

5. To maintain ethical standards in all trading activities

6. To represent the trading profession positively

7. To use trading profits wisely and responsibly

8. To maintain physical and mental health for optimal performance

9. To contribute to the trading community's knowledge base

10. To leave the trading world better than you found it

The Ultimate Stop-Loss

The Graduation Ceremony: Your Commitment to Excellence

The Master Trader's Oath

Stand and repeat:

"I, [your name], having completed my study of stop loss mastery, do hereby commit to:

- Place all stops at the last low when buying and last high when selling

- Never move stops against my position under any circumstances

- Size all positions based on stop distance and predetermined risk

- Risk only amounts I can afford to lose without emotional distress

- Maintain patience and discipline under all market conditions

- Continue learning and growing throughout my trading career

- Share my knowledge generously with other developing traders

- Use my trading profits wisely to build lasting wealth

- Maintain integrity and ethical standards in all trading activities

- Honor these commitments even when challenged by difficult circumstances

I understand that mastery is not a destination but a journey of continuous improvement. I pledge to uphold these principles and represent the highest standards of the trading profession.

So I commit, and so I shall trade."

Your Graduation Certificate

Certificate of Stop Loss Mastery

This certifies that **[Your Name]** has successfully completed the comprehensive study of stop loss mastery and demonstrated understanding of:

The Ultimate Stop-Loss

- Primary and secondary stop placement rules

- Position sizing and risk management principles

- Multiple timeframe analysis and market session awareness

- Scaling strategies and advanced position management

- Psychological mastery and discipline development

- Integration with complete trading systems

Having shown dedication to learning these principles and commitment to applying them consistently, **[Your Name]** is hereby recognized as having achieved **Stop Loss Mastery** and is prepared to build lasting wealth through disciplined trading.

Awarded this day: _____

Your signature: _____

Your Personal Hall of Fame

Document Your Achievement:

- Date you completed your mastery study

- Key insights that transformed your trading

- Mentors and teachers who helped your development

- Students you've helped along their journey

- Milestones achieved through disciplined application

- Goals for continued growth and contribution

Final Words: Your Journey Continues

The End is the Beginning

You've reached the end of this book but the beginning of your mastery journey. The principles you've learned will serve you for decades to come. They will

The Ultimate Stop-Loss

make you money in bull markets and protect you in bear markets. They will give you confidence during uncertainty and peace of mind during volatility.

Your Unique Contribution

No one else will apply these principles exactly as you do. Your personality, experience, and insights will create a unique expression of stop loss mastery. This uniqueness is valuable—it's what you'll share with others who follow your path.

The Ripple Effect

Every trader you help, every principle you share, every example you set creates ripples that extend far beyond your direct influence. Your mastery contributes to a trading community built on discipline, integrity, and mutual support.

The Ultimate Success

True success in trading isn't measured only by the money you make—it's measured by the trader you become in the process. The character you develop, the disciplines you master, and the contributions you make define your ultimate success.

Chapter 20 Summary: Your Success Principles

Your journey to stop loss mastery concludes with these eternal principles:

1. **Follow the Ten Commandments:** These principles are your unwavering guide

2. **Build Character:** Develop patience, discipline, humility, resilience, and integrity

3. **Create Wealth Systematically:** Use trading as the foundation for lasting financial success

4. **Teach Others:** Share your knowledge and help build the next generation

5. **Never Stop Growing:** Mastery is a journey, not a destination

The Ultimate Stop-Loss

6. **Make Your Commitment:** Take the oath and honor it throughout your career

You now possess one of trading's most valuable skills. Use it wisely, share it generously, and build upon it continuously. The market will reward your discipline, and the trading community will benefit from your contribution.

Welcome to the ranks of truly skilled traders. Your journey to mastery is complete—your journey to greatness has just begun.

Trade well. Trade disciplined. Trade with mastery.

ACKNOWLEDGMENTS

First and foremost, I want to thank every student of Royalty FX Academy who trusted the process before the results were proven. Your willingness to think differently and embrace higher timeframe stop placement, even when it felt uncomfortable, provided the real-world validation for this methodology.

To my early students who endured my trial-and-error period as I refined these concepts—thank you for your patience and feedback. Your questions forced me to clarify my thinking and develop better explanations.

Special thanks to [Student Name] and [Student Name], whose trading journals provided many of the case studies in this book. Your willingness to share both your struggles and successes will help thousands of future traders avoid the same pitfalls.

To my mentor [Mentor Name], who first taught me that "wide stops with small positions beat tight stops with large positions every time." That simple phrase changed my entire approach to risk management.

To my family, who supported me through countless late nights developing the Royalty FX Academy curriculum and writing this collection. Your understanding when I missed dinners because "the London session was too good to miss" means everything.

Finally, to every trader who has ever been stopped out by a few pips only to watch their analysis play out perfectly—this book is my gift to you. May you never experience that frustration again.

ABOUT ROYALTY FX ACADEMY

MISSION STATEMENT Royalty FX Academy exists to transform struggling traders into consistently profitable ones by teaching higher timeframe analysis, disciplined risk management, and the psychology of patience.

OUR PHILOSOPHY We believe that successful trading is 80% psychology and 20% technique. Most trading education focuses exclusively on the 20%, leaving students technically competent but psychologically unprepared. At Royalty FX Academy, we address both components equally.

OUR APPROACH

- **Higher Timeframe Focus:** We only trade setups that originate from monthly, weekly, or daily timeframes

- **Simple Price Action:** We use only engulfing bar patterns—nothing else

- **Proper Risk Management:** We place stops based on market structure, not fear

- **Patient Execution:** We enter trades on the 4-hour timeframe and wait for results

THE MASTERY COLLECTION The Royalty FX Academy Mastery Collection represents over five years of curriculum development and real-world testing. Each book builds upon the previous one, creating a complete trading education system:

1. **Psychology** - The mental foundation for trading success

2. **The Only Price Action You Will Ever Need** - Mastering engulfing bars

3. **Mastering the Bearish Forest** - Complete selling methodology

4. **The Ultimate Buying Setup** - Complete buying methodology

5. **Volume 1: Selling Workbook** - Hands-on selling practice

6. **Volume 2: Buying Workbook** - Hands-on buying practice

The Ultimate Stop-Loss

7. **Stop Loss Placement** - Risk management mastery

8. **Beyond Basics** - Complete compilation and advanced concepts

STUDENT RESULTS Our methodology has been tested by over [X,XXX] students worldwide, with a documented success rate of [XX]% achieving consistent profitability within their first year of implementation.

CONTACT INFORMATION Website: www.royaltyfxacademy.com Social Media: @_RoyaltyFXAcademy_

ABOUT THE AUTHOR

[Your Name] is the founder and head instructor of Royalty FX Academy, a leading forex education institution focused on higher timeframe analysis and psychological trading development.

TRADING BACKGROUND [Your Name] began trading forex in [Year], initially struggling like most new traders with inconsistent results and emotional decision-making. After years of trial and error, multiple account blow-ups, and countless hours of market analysis, he developed the higher timeframe methodology that would become the foundation of Royalty FX Academy.

The breakthrough came during the expensive lesson described in this book's prologue—a 2:47 AM realization that proper stop placement was the missing piece in his trading puzzle. This discovery led to [X] consecutive years of profitable trading and the development of the systematic approach taught at Royalty FX Academy.

TEACHING PHILOSOPHY "Most traders fail not because they lack technical knowledge, but because they lack the psychology to implement what they know. My job is to build both the technical foundation and the mental discipline required for long-term success."

ACHIEVEMENTS

- Founder of Royalty FX Academy ([Year])

- Author of 8 books in the Mastery Collection

- Mentor to over 200 students worldwide

- Developer of the Higher Timeframe Trading Methodology

- [Any other relevant achievements, certifications, or recognition]

PERSONAL When not analyzing charts or teaching students, [Your Name] enjoys [personal interests/hobbies]. He currently resides in [Location] and continues to trade his own account using the exact methodology taught in his courses.

The Ultimate Stop-Loss

PHILOSOPHY "Trading is the ultimate test of self-discipline. Master yourself, and the markets will follow."

BIBLIOGRAPHY/REFERENCES

TRADING CLASSICS THAT INFLUENCED THIS METHODOLOGY

Buffett, Warren. *The Intelligent Investor*. Various interviews and annual letters.

Douglas, Mark. *Trading in the Zone: Master the Market with Confidence, Discipline, and a Winning Attitude*. New York Institute of Finance, 2000.

Elder, Alexander. *Trading for a Living: Psychology, Trading Tactics, Money Management*. John Wiley & Sons, 1993.

Livermore, Jesse. *Reminiscences of a Stock Operator*. Originally published 1923.

Schwager, Jack D. *Market Wizards: Interviews with Top Traders*. Harper Business, 1989.

Tharp, Van K. *Trade Your Way to Financial Freedom*. McGraw-Hill, 2006.

RISK MANAGEMENT STUDIES [Academic papers or studies on risk management, if any were referenced]

MARKET STRUCTURE ANALYSIS [Any technical analysis books or resources that influenced your approach]

Note: This methodology was developed through personal experience, student feedback, and years of market observation rather than academic study. The references listed represent influential works that shaped the psychological and risk management foundations of the Royalty FX Academy approach.

The Ultimate Stop-Loss
📑 INDEX

The Ultimate Stop-Loss

OTHER BOOKS IN THE MASTERY COLLECTION

COMPLETE YOUR FOREX EDUCATION WITH THE FULL ROYALTY FX ACADEMY MASTERY COLLECTION

Book 1: Psychology - The Mental Foundation Master the psychological aspects of trading that determine 80% of your success. Learn to control emotions, develop discipline, and build the mindset of a consistent winner.

Book 2: The Only Price Action You Will Ever Need Everything you need to know about engulfing bar patterns. This is the foundation for all Royalty FX Academy strategies—master this before moving to advanced concepts.

Book 3: Mastering the Bearish Forest Complete methodology for selling the market. Learn to identify bearish setups from higher timeframes and execute them with precision on the 4-hour chart.

Book 4: The Ultimate Buying Setup Your complete guide to buying the market. Discover how to spot bullish opportunities and enter them at the optimal time for maximum profit potential.

Book 5: Volume 1 - Selling Workbook Hands-on practice for selling strategies. Step-by-step exercises teach you to draw zones, identify trend lines, and perfect your bearish market analysis.

Book 6: Volume 2 - Buying Workbook Practical application for buying setups. Interactive exercises that build your skills in bullish market identification and trend analysis.

Book 7: Stop Loss Placement *(You are here)* The missing piece in most traders' education. Learn proper risk management through higher timeframe stop placement techniques.

Book 8: Beyond Basics - The Complete Compilation All seven books combined into one comprehensive reference, plus advanced concepts and strategies for experienced traders.

The Ultimate Stop-Loss

SPECIAL COLLECTION PRICING Save 40% when you purchase the complete 8-book Mastery Collection Visit: www.royaltyfxacademy.com/mastery-collection

---

CONTACT INFORMATION & RESOURCES

ROYALTY FX ACADEMY HEADQUARTERS [Your Business Address] [City, State, ZIP Code] [Country]

CONTACT Email: royaltyfxacademy@gmail.com Website: www.royaltyfxacademy.com

SOCIAL MEDIA Facebook: @RoyaltyFXAcademy Instagram: @_RoyaltyFXAcademy_
Twitter: @RoyaltyFXAcademy YouTube: Royalty FX Academy Channel

ADDITIONAL RESOURCES

FREE RESOURCES:

- Weekly market analysis videos
- Monthly trading webinars
- Student success stories
- Trading psychology articles

PREMIUM COURSES:

- Live Trading Room Access
- One-on-One Mentoring Programs
- Advanced Strategy Workshops
- Psychology Mastery Course

STUDENT SUPPORT:

- Private Student Facebook Group
- Weekly Q&A Sessions
- Email Support (48-hour response guarantee)
- Trading Journal Review Service

The Ultimate Stop-Loss

CERTIFICATION PROGRAMS:

- Royalty FX Academy Certified Trader

- Advanced Psychology Certification

- Mentorship Training Program

PARTNERSHIP OPPORTUNITIES:

- Affiliate Program

- Educational Institution Partnerships

- Corporate Training Programs

For the latest updates, course offerings, and market analysis, visit our website or follow us on social media.

The Ultimate Stop-Loss
AFTERWORD

THE JOURNEY CONTINUES

As you close this book, you're not ending a learning experience—you're beginning a transformation.

The methodology you've learned represents more than just technical analysis or risk management rules. It represents a fundamental shift in how you think about trading, about patience, and about success itself.

Most traders spend their entire careers fighting the market, trying to impose their will on price action, desperately seeking the perfect entry signal that will make them rich overnight. They focus on being right instead of being profitable. They choose comfort over growth, speed over sustainability, hope over discipline.

You now have the tools to be different.

You understand that proper stop placement isn't just about protecting capital—it's about protecting psychology. You know that higher timeframes aren't just about finding better setups—they're about finding peace of mind. You've learned that patience isn't just a virtue—it's a competitive advantage.

But knowledge without application is worthless. The real test begins now.

YOUR COMMITMENT

I challenge you to make a commitment—not just to the methodology, but to yourself:

- Commit to placing every stop loss according to the hierarchy you've learned

- Commit to trusting higher timeframe analysis even when it feels uncomfortable

- Commit to being patient even when others are rushing

The Ultimate Stop-Loss

- Commit to small positions with proper stops instead of large positions with tight stops

- Commit to measuring success by process, not just by profit

THE COMPOUND EFFECT

Remember that trading success compounds. Each properly placed stop builds confidence. Each patient trade develops discipline. Each higher timeframe analysis strengthens your market understanding.

You don't need to be perfect immediately. You just need to be better than you were yesterday, and better today than you'll be tomorrow.

The Ultimate Stop-Loss
A FINAL THOUGHT

Years from now, when you're consistently profitable and other traders ask for your secret, you'll tell them about stop loss placement. They'll look at you strangely, expecting some complex indicator or mysterious pattern.

But you'll know the truth: the difference between struggling traders and successful ones isn't found in exotic strategies or insider knowledge. It's found in the willingness to do simple things consistently, even when they feel uncomfortable.

Welcome to that select group.

The market is waiting for you—not to conquer it, but to dance with it.

Trade with honor. Trade with discipline. Trade like royalty.

[Your Name] Founder, Royalty FX Academy

"Success in trading isn't about predicting the future—it's about managing the present."